WILLIAM SHAKESPEARE

As You Like It

Edited with a Commentary by
H. J. OLIVER
and with an Introduction by
KATHERINE DUNCAN-JONES

PENGUIN BOOKS

PENGUIN CLASSICS

UK | USA | Canada | Ireland | Australia
India | New Zealand | South Africa

Penguin Books is part of the Penguin Random House group of companies
whose addresses can be found at global.penguinrandomhouse.com.

This edition first published in Penguin Books 1968
Reissued in the Penguin Shakespeare series 2005
Reissued in Penguin Classics 2015

001

Set in PostScript Monotype Fournier
Typeset by Palimpsest Book Productions Limited, Falkirk, Stirlingshire
Printed in Great Britain by Clays Ltd, St Ives plc

ISBN: 978–0–141–39627–9

www.greenpenguin.co.uk

MIX
Paper from
responsible sources
FSC
www.fsc.org   FSC® C018179

Penguin Random House is committed to a
sustainable future for our business, our readers
and our planet. This book is made from Forest
Stewardship Council® certified paper.

FOUNDING EDITOR: T. J. B. SPENCER
STANLEY WELLS
SUPERVISORY EDITORS: PAUL EDMONDSON, STANLEY WELLS

AS YOU LIKE IT

T. J. B. SPENCER, sometime Director of the Shakespeare Institute of the University of Birmingham, was the founding editor of the New Penguin Shakespeare, for which he edited both *Romeo and Juliet* and *Hamlet*.

STANLEY WELLS is Honorary President of the Shakespeare Birthplace Trust, Emeritus Professor of Shakespeare Studies in the University of Birmingham, and General Editor of the Oxford Shakespeare. His many books include *Shakespeare: For All Time*, *Shakespeare & Co.*, *Shakespeare, Sex, and Love* and *Great Shakespeare Actors*.

H. J. OLIVER was Professor of English at the University of New South Wales. He edited *The Merry Wives of Windsor* and *Timon of Athens* for the Arden Shakespeare and *The Taming of the Shrew* for the Oxford Shakespeare.

KATHERINE DUNCAN-JONES is a Fellow of Somerville College, Oxford. She has written biographies of Sidney (*Sir Philip Sidney: Courtier Poet*) and of Shakespeare (*Ungentle Shakespeare: Scenes from his Life*), and has edited *Shakespeare's Sonnets* for the Arden Shakespeare. She has also edited Shakespeare's *Poems* for Arden.

Contents

General Introduction

Every play by Shakespeare is unique. This is part of his greatness. A restless and indefatigable experimenter, he moved with a rare amalgamation of artistic integrity and dedicated professionalism from one kind of drama to another. Never shackled by convention, he offered his actors the alternation between serious and comic modes from play to play, and often also within the plays themselves, that the repertory system within which he worked demanded, and which provided an invaluable stimulus to his imagination. Introductions to individual works in this series attempt to define their individuality. But there are common factors that underpin Shakespeare's career.

Nothing in his heredity offers clues to the origins of his genius. His upbringing in Stratford-upon-Avon, where he was born in 1564, was unexceptional. His mother, born Mary Arden, came from a prosperous farming family. Her father chose her as his executor over her eight sisters and his four stepchildren when she was only in her late teens, which suggests that she was of more than average practical ability. Her husband John, a glover, apparently unable to write, was nevertheless a capable businessman and loyal townsfellow, who seems to have fallen on relatively hard times in later life. He would have been brought up as a Catholic, and may have retained

Catholic sympathies, but his son subscribed publicly to Anglicanism throughout his life.

The most important formative influence on Shakespeare was his school. As the son of an alderman who became bailiff (or mayor) in 1568, he had the right to attend the town's grammar school. Here he would have received an education grounded in classical rhetoric and oratory, studying authors such as Ovid, Cicero and Quintilian, and would have been required to read, speak, write and even think in Latin from his early years. This classical education permeates Shakespeare's work from the beginning to the end of his career. It is apparent in the self-conscious classicism of plays of the early 1590s such as the tragedy of *Titus Andronicus*, *The Comedy of Errors*, and the narrative poems *Venus and Adonis* (1592–3) and *The Rape of Lucrece* (1593–4), and is still evident in his latest plays, informing the dream visions of *Pericles* and *Cymbeline* and the masque in *The Tempest*, written between 1607 and 1611. It inflects his literary style throughout his career. In his earliest writings the verse, based on the ten-syllabled, five-beat iambic pentameter, is highly patterned. Rhetorical devices deriving from classical literature, such as alliteration and antithesis, extended similes and elaborate wordplay, abound. Often, as in *Love's Labour's Lost* and *A Midsummer Night's Dream*, he uses rhyming patterns associated with lyric poetry, each line self-contained in sense, the prose as well as the verse employing elaborate figures of speech. Writing at a time of linguistic ferment, Shakespeare frequently imports Latinisms into English, coining words such as abstemious, addiction, incarnadine and adjunct. He was also heavily influenced by the eloquent translations of the Bible in both the Bishops' and the Geneva versions. As his experience grows, his verse and prose become more supple,

the patterning less apparent, more ready to accommo-
date the rhythms of ordinary speech, more colloquial in
diction, as in the speeches of the Nurse in *Romeo and
Juliet*, the characterful prose of Falstaff and Hamlet's
soliloquies. The effect is of increasing psychological
realism, reaching its greatest heights in *Hamlet*, *Othello*,
King Lear, *Macbeth* and *Antony and Cleopatra*. Gradually
he discovered ways of adapting the regular beat of the
pentameter to make it an infinitely flexible instrument for
matching thought with feeling. Towards the end of his
career, in plays such as *The Winter's Tale*, *Cymbeline* and
The Tempest, he adopts a more highly mannered style,
in keeping with the more overtly symbolical and emblem-
atical mode in which he is writing.

So far as we know, Shakespeare lived in Stratford till
after his marriage to Anne Hathaway, eight years his
senior, in 1582. They had three children: a daughter,
Susanna, born in 1583 within six months of their marriage,
and twins, Hamnet and Judith, born in 1585. The next
seven years of Shakespeare's life are virtually a blank.
Theories that he may have been, for instance, a school-
master, or a lawyer, or a soldier, or a sailor, lack evidence
to support them. The first reference to him in print, in
Robert Greene's pamphlet *Greene's Groatsworth of Wit*
of 1592, parodies a line from *Henry VI, Part III*, implying
that Shakespeare was already an established playwright.
It seems likely that at some unknown point after the birth
of his twins he joined a theatre company and gained
experience as both actor and writer in the provinces and
London. The London theatres closed because of plague
in 1593 and 1594; and during these years, perhaps recog-
nizing the need for an alternative career, he wrote and
published the narrative poems *Venus and Adonis* and *The
Rape of Lucrece*. These are the only works we can be

certain that Shakespeare himself was responsible for putting into print. Each bears the author's dedication to Henry Wriothesley, Earl of Southampton (1573–1624), the second in warmer terms than the first. Southampton, younger than Shakespeare by ten years, is the only person to whom he personally dedicated works. The Earl may have been a close friend, perhaps even the beautiful and adored young man whom Shakespeare celebrates in his *Sonnets*.

The resumption of playing after the plague years saw the founding of the Lord Chamberlain's Men, a company to which Shakespeare was to belong for the rest of his career, as actor, shareholder and playwright. No other dramatist of the period had so stable a relationship with a single company. Shakespeare knew the actors for whom he was writing and the conditions in which they performed. The permanent company was made up of around twelve to fourteen players, but one actor often played more than one role in a play and additional actors were hired as needed. Led by the tragedian Richard Burbage (1568–1619) and, initially, the comic actor Will Kemp (d. 1603), they rapidly achieved a high reputation, and when King James I succeeded Queen Elizabeth I in 1603 they were renamed as the King's Men. All the women's parts were played by boys; there is no evidence that any female role was ever played by a male actor over the age of about eighteen. Shakespeare had enough confidence in his boys to write for them long and demanding roles such as Rosalind (who, like other heroines of the romantic comedies, is disguised as a boy for much of the action) in *As You Like It*, Lady Macbeth and Cleopatra. But there are far more fathers than mothers, sons than daughters, in his plays, few if any of which require more than the company's normal complement of three or four boys.

The company played primarily in London's public playhouses – there were almost none that we know of in the rest of the country – initially in the Theatre, built in Shoreditch in 1576, and from 1599 in the Globe, on Bankside. These were wooden, more or less circular structures, open to the air, with a thrust stage surmounted by a canopy and jutting into the area where spectators who paid one penny stood, and surrounded by galleries where it was possible to be seated on payment of an additional penny. Though properties such as cauldrons, stocks, artificial trees or beds could indicate locality, there was no representational scenery. Sound effects such as flourishes of trumpets, music both martial and amorous, and accompaniments to songs were provided by the company's musicians. Actors entered through doors in the back wall of the stage. Above it was a balconied area that could represent the walls of a town (as in *King John*), or a castle (as in *Richard II*), and indeed a balcony (as in *Romeo and Juliet*). In 1609 the company also acquired the use of the Blackfriars, a smaller, indoor theatre to which admission was more expensive, and which permitted the use of more spectacular stage effects such as the descent of Jupiter on an eagle in *Cymbeline* and of goddesses in *The Tempest*. And they would frequently perform before the court in royal residences and, on their regular tours into the provinces, in non-theatrical spaces such as inns, guild-halls and the great halls of country houses.

Early in his career Shakespeare may have worked in collaboration, perhaps with Thomas Nashe (1567–*c*. 1601) in *Henry VI, Part I* and with George Peele (1556–96) in *Titus Andronicus*. And towards the end he collaborated with George Wilkins (*fl.* 1604–8) in *Pericles*, and with his younger colleagues Thomas Middleton (1580–1627), in *Timon of Athens*, and John Fletcher (1579–1625), in *Henry*

VIII, *The Two Noble Kinsmen* and the lost play *Cardenio*. Shakespeare's output dwindled in his last years, and he died in 1616 in Stratford, where he owned a fine house, New Place, and much land. His only son had died at the age of eleven, in 1596, and his last descendant died in 1670. New Place was destroyed in the eighteenth century but the other Stratford houses associated with his life are maintained and displayed to the public by the Shakespeare Birthplace Trust.

One of the most remarkable features of Shakespeare's plays is their intellectual and emotional scope. They span a great range from the lightest of comedies, such as *The Two Gentlemen of Verona* and *The Comedy of Errors*, to the profoundest of tragedies, such as *King Lear* and *Macbeth*. He maintained an output of around two plays a year, ringing the changes between comic and serious. All his comedies have serious elements: Shylock, in *The Merchant of Venice*, almost reaches tragic dimensions, and *Measure for Measure* is profoundly serious in its examination of moral problems. Equally, none of his tragedies is without humour: Hamlet is as witty as any of his comic heroes, *Macbeth* has its Porter, and *King Lear* its Fool. His greatest comic character, Falstaff, inhabits the history plays and *Henry V* ends with a marriage, while *Henry VI, Part III*, *Richard II* and *Richard III* culminate in the tragic deaths of their protagonists.

Although in performance Shakespeare's characters can give the impression of a superabundant reality, he is not a naturalistic dramatist. None of his plays is explicitly set in his own time. The action of few of them (except for the English histories) is set even partly in England (exceptions are *The Merry Wives of Windsor* and the Induction to *The Taming of the Shrew*). Italy is his favoured location. Most of his principal story-lines derive from printed writings; but the structuring and translation of these narratives into dramatic terms is Shakespeare's own, and he invents much additional material. Most of the plays contain elements of myth and legend, and many derive from ancient or more recent history or from romantic tales of ancient times and faraway places. All reflect his reading, often in close detail. Holinshed's *Chronicles* (1577, revised 1587), a great compendium of English, Scottish and Irish history, provided material for his English history plays. The *Lives of the Noble Grecians and Romans* by the Greek writer Plutarch, finely translated into English from the French by Sir Thomas North in 1579, provided much of the narrative material, and also a mass of verbal detail, for his plays about Roman history. Some plays are closely based on shorter individual works: *As You Like It*, for instance, on the novel *Rosalynde* (1590) by his near-contemporary Thomas Lodge (1558–1625), *The Winter's Tale* on *Pandosto* (1588) by his old rival Robert Greene (1558–92) and *Othello* on a story by the Italian Giraldi Cinthio (1504–73). And the language of his plays is permeated by the Bible, the Book of Common Prayer and the proverbial sayings of his day.

Shakespeare was popular with his contemporaries, but his commitment to the theatre and to the plays in performance is demonstrated by the fact that only about half of his plays appeared in print in his lifetime, in slim paperback volumes known as quartos, so called because they were made from printers' sheets folded twice to form four leaves (eight pages). None of them shows any sign that he was involved in their publication. For him, performance was the primary means of publication. The most frequently reprinted of his works were the non-dramatic poems – the erotic *Venus and Adonis* and the more moralistic *The Rape of Lucrece*. The *Sonnets*, which appeared in 1609, under his name but possibly without his consent, were less successful, perhaps because the vogue for sonnet sequences, which peaked in the 1590s, had passed by then. They were not reprinted until 1640, and then only in garbled form along with poems by other writers. Happily, in 1623, seven years after he died, his colleagues John Heminges (1556–1630) and Henry Condell (d. 1627) published his collected plays, including eighteen that had not previously appeared in print, in the first Folio, whose name derives from the fact that the printers' sheets were folded only once to produce two leaves (four pages). Some of the quarto editions are badly printed, and the fact that some plays exist in two, or even three, early versions creates problems for editors. These are discussed in the Account of the Text in each volume of this series.

Shakespeare's plays continued in the repertoire until the Puritans closed the theatres in 1642. When performances resumed after the Restoration of the monarchy in 1660 many of the plays were not to the taste of the times, especially because their mingling of genres and failure to meet the requirements of poetic justice offended against the dictates of neoclassicism. Some, such as *The Tempest* (changed by John Dryden and William Davenant in 1667 to suit contemporary taste), *King Lear* (to which Nahum Tate gave a happy ending in 1681) and *Richard III* (heavily adapted by Colley Cibber in 1700 as a vehicle for his own talents), were extensively rewritten; others fell into neglect. Slowly they regained their place in the repertoire, and they continued to be reprinted, but it was not until the great actor David Garrick (1717–79) organized a spectacular jubilee in Stratford in 1769 that Shakespeare began to be regarded as a transcendental genius. Garrick's idolatry prefigured the enthusiasm of critics such as Samuel Taylor Coleridge (1772–1834) and William Hazlitt (1778–1830). Gradually Shakespeare's reputation spread abroad, to Germany, America, France and to other European countries.

During the nineteenth century, though the plays were generally still performed in heavily adapted or abbreviated versions, a large body of scholarship and criticism began to amass. Partly as a result of a general swing in education away from the teaching of Greek and Roman texts and towards literature written in English, Shakespeare became the object of intensive study in schools and universities. In the theatre, important turning points were the work in England of two theatre directors, William Poel (1852–1934) and his disciple Harley Granville-Barker (1877–1946), who showed that the application of knowledge, some of it newly acquired, of early staging conditions to performance of the plays could render the original texts viable in terms of the modern theatre. During the twentieth century appreciation of Shakespeare's work, encouraged by the availability of audio, film and video versions of the plays, spread around the world to such an extent that he can now be claimed as a global author.

The influence of Shakespeare's works permeates the English language. Phrases from his plays and poems – 'a tower of strength', 'green-eyed jealousy', 'a foregone conclusion' – are on the lips of people who may never have read him. They have inspired composers of songs, orchestral music and operas; painters and sculptors; poets, novelists and film-makers. Allusions to him appear in pop songs, in advertisements and in television shows. Some of his characters – Romeo and Juliet, Falstaff, Shylock and Hamlet – have acquired mythic status. He is valued for his humanity, his psychological insight, his wit and humour, his lyricism, his mastery of language, his ability to excite, surprise, move and, in the widest sense of the word, entertain audiences. He is the greatest of poets, but he is essentially a dramatic poet. Though his plays have much to offer to readers, they exist fully only in performance. In these volumes we offer individual introductions, notes on language and on specific points of the text, suggestions for further reading and information about how each work has been edited. In addition we include accounts of the ways in which successive generations of interpreters and audiences have responded to challenges and rewards offered by the plays. The Penguin Shakespeare series aspires to remove obstacles to understanding and to make pleasurable the reading of the work of the man who has done more than most to make us understand what it is to be human.

Stanley Wells

The Chronology of
Shakespeare's Works

A few of Shakespeare's writings can be fairly precisely dated. An allusion to the Earl of Essex in the chorus to Act V of *Henry V*, for instance, could only have been written in 1599. But for many of the plays we have only vague information, such as the date of publication, which may have occurred long after composition, the date of a performance, which may not have been the first, or a list in Francis Meres's book *Palladis Tamia*, published in 1598, which tells us only that the plays listed there must have been written by that year. The chronology of the early plays is particularly difficult to establish. Not everyone would agree that the first part of *Henry VI* was written after the third, for instance, or *Romeo and Juliet* before *A Midsummer Night's Dream*. The following table is based on the 'Canon and Chronology' section in *William Shakespeare: A Textual Companion*, by Stanley Wells and Gary Taylor, with John Jowett and William Montgomery (1987), where more detailed information and discussion may be found.

The Two Gentlemen of Verona	1590–91
The Taming of the Shrew	1590–91
Henry VI, Part II	1591
Henry VI, Part III	1591

Introduction

'TO LIBERTY, AND
NOT TO BANISHMENT'

As its title promises, *As You Like It* is one of Shake-speare's most accessible and enjoyable comedies. Its pace is rapid, and the complexities of its plot are lightly handled. There may be no very good reason why the young hero Orlando should discuss his life story with an old family servant in the play's opening speech, which begins:

> As I remember, Adam, it was upon this fashion bequeathed me by will, but poor a thousand crowns, and, as thou sayest, charged my brother on his blessing to breed me well; and there begins my sadness.

But this is an efficient and painless way of telling the audience the story so far. The speech also establishes immediate sympathy for young Orlando, who has been so badly treated by the elder brother, who has denied him both money and education. Many of Shakespeare's other comedies have 'romantic' heroes who seem worryingly unworthy of the girls who love them, and whom they are destined to marry. In the early *The Two Gentlemen of*

Verona, for instance, the unfaithful and unpleasant Proteus seems wholly unsuitable for Julia. The shallow Claudio hardly deserves to win the patient and demure Hero in *Much Ado About Nothing*, especially since he never apologizes adequately for his cruel, near-fatal treatment of her. Unusually, Orlando is a thoroughly likeable and good-natured young man. Despite his lack of formal education he has virtues of instinctive loyalty and courage that make him seem worthy of being loved by Rosalind. Also, though he is the youngest, he seems to be the truest son of his dead father Sir Rowland de Boys. The fact that we have already been drawn into sympathy with the good-hearted and ill-used Orlando lends additional excitement to the two fights that command our attention in Act I, even though in the first one, Orlando's scuffle with his elder brother Oliver (I.1.49–69), he is the aggressor. By the time we witness the second fight, Orlando's public wrestling match with the thuggish Charles (I.2.199–208), we shall have become, as audience, enthusiastic supporters of the wronged youth. Act I establishes the court of the usurper Duke Frederick as a thoroughly unpleasant place in which bullies and sadists flourish. It also introduces us to five of the principal characters, Orlando, Adam, Rosalind, Celia and Touchstone, all of whom escape from it into the Forest of Arden.

Most of Shakespeare's comedies become fully comic, fully happy for characters and audience alike, only in their closing moments. In *As You Like It*, however, this change occurs very much earlier. At the beginning of Act II we see the banished Duke Senior, who has been expelled and replaced by his ruthless younger brother Duke Frederick, surrounded by *'two or three Lords dressed like foresters'*, and thoroughly enjoying himself. From this moment on, the tone of rest of the play is established.

After opening scenes focused on the cruelty and gratuitous violence at the court of Duke Frederick, where
brothers are brutally unkind to brothers and 'the breaking
of ribs' is offered as 'sport for ladies' (I.2.128–9), all the
rest of the play is one long celebration of benign comic
freedom. The banished Duke praises the special sweet-
ness of life in the Forest of Arden, in which all the forces
that normally generate pain are transformed either into
sources of pleasure or occasions for laughter. He himself,
now that he lives in a forest rather than a palace, takes
the most pleasure in being liberated from the falsity and
treachery of life at court. The cold winds that blow on
him do so without flattery, malice or deceit: 'This is no
flattery; these are counsellors | That feelingly persuade
me what I am' (II.1.10–11). The remote greenwood,
'exempt from public haunt' (15), is the perfect environment for the life of virtuous contemplation that he most
enjoys, enabling him to find 'Sermons in stones, and
good in everything' (17). As his niece Celia remarks at
the close of the first act, the journey from the French
court to the forest leads everyone 'To liberty, and not to
banishment' (I.3.136).

The pleasures of retired contemplation in remote
woodlands were a commonplace of Elizabethan courtly
literature. This was a period during which all kinds of
pastoral writing flourished, some of it highly artificial,
some of it suggesting genuine delight in country life. In
the prose and verse romance *Arcadia* by Philip Sidney
(1554–86), for instance, one of the two princely heroes
composes an elaborate song beginning:

> O sweet woods, the delight of solitariness!
> O how much I do like your solitariness!

He goes on to praise the woods especially for the absence from them of 'treason', 'envy' and 'flatterers' venomous insinuations'. Sidney's poem was adapted into a lute-song by John Dowland in his *Booke of Songes and Ayres* published in 1600, which belongs to the very same period as Shakespeare's play, a period in which retirement from the seat of government appeared extremely appealing. More will be said later about the political reasons for this. In *As You Like It* the exiles from court who discover liberty in banishment include Duke Senior's daughter Rosalind as well as her friend and cousin Celia and the court jester Touchstone, a character added by Shakespeare to his source in Thomas Lodge's popular romance *Rosalynde*, first printed in 1590. For Rosalind, the forest offers not merely release from her existence as an unwelcome misfit at the court of the tyrannical Duke Frederick but an opportunity to escape the restrictions of life as a young woman. By dressing herself in 'all points like a man' (I.3.114) she liberates herself not only to travel safely but, more crucially, to speak openly and fully. Indeed, she/he speaks more lines than any other woman in Shakespeare's plays. In her male role as 'Ganymede' she discovers the pleasure and amusement of manipulating other people, both men and women. She controls them through a succession of verbal games. And though her companion Celia plays a subordinate role, she, too, gains considerable autonomy as a landowner and mistress of a farm, as well as acting as Rosalind's affectionate and sometimes slightly critical confidante. In the play's first edition, in the 1623 first Folio, their affable companion is always called 'Clown' in speech headings and stage directions. However, on arrival in the forest he becomes an eccentric gentleman, 'Master Touchstone'. As a worldly man freshly arrived

from court he can lord it over the rustic 'clown' Corin
(II.4) as well as over his sexual rival, the simple-minded
William (V.1).

For the young romantic hero Orlando, the Forest of
Arden has even more to offer. It provides an environment within which his natural goodness can be recog-
nized and honoured despite his poverty and lack of
education, and where he can receive – under the guise
of play-acting – just that training in 'gentleness' that was
denied to him by his eldest brother. In other romantic
comedies one of the most nagging sources of pain for
the younger characters is unrequited love. But here even
that is converted into pleasure and entertainment. Both
Rosalind and Orlando go through the motions of suffering from love melancholy, but in neither case does
their melancholy trouble them for very long. Though
Rosalind complains to Celia about the pains of falling
in love, hopelessly and at first sight – 'O, how full of
briars is this working-day world!' (I.3.11–12) – she
quickly cheers up at the prospect of disguise and adventure. Arrived in Arden she immediately recognizes the
lovesick shepherd Silvius as suffering from just the same
complaint as herself: 'Jove, Jove! This shepherd's passion |
Is much upon my fashion' (II.4.55–6). It seems that by
ridiculing lovesickness in others – both in Silvius and in
her very own Orlando – she uses these young men as a
kind of emotional safety valve, effectively displacing her
own pain by converting the miseries of unrequited love
into a source of unending merriment.

Orlando, too, suffers at first from love melancholy.
His poignant and lyrical soliloquy at the beginning of
Act III, scene 2, which is almost a sonnet in form, suggests
that he anticipates a protracted commitment to lonely
chastity and unrequited love. Yet he soon discovers that

he is by no means too miserable to engage in some rough banter with Jaques (III.2.246–86) before subjecting himself to sustained raillery from 'Ganymede'. His eager compliance with Ganymede's plan to cure him of love – or rather, to train him to perform the part of a lover correctly – suggests that at some level he fully understands that the real point of being in the Forest of Arden is to 'fleet the time carelessly' (I.1.111–12), and to take pleasure in the here and now without any regard to serious goals or practicalities. The capacity of both Rosalind and Orlando to convert love melancholy into a pastime and a performance, rather than a source of pain, sets them apart from Silvius and Phebe, the amorous shepherd and disdainful shepherdess, whose sufferings are found so ridiculous by the characters who witness them. While Rosalind and Orlando achieve, or pretend to achieve, a coolly ironic distance from the passion that drives them, Silvius achieves none. Yet the earnestness with which he pursues his 'Sweet Phebe' is not only comic; it can also be extremely appealing in performance. There have been several modern productions of the play in which the unironic, uncool Silvius has come surprisingly close to upstaging the much more sophisticated Orlando.

Many other apparently disturbing themes are handled comically. For instance, it is normally implied in romantic comedy that marriage will resolve all difficulties once the partners are matched in accordance with their own desires. We are not generally encouraged to speculate about anything that may go wrong once the marriage has been solemnized. All is assumed to be well as the couples dance their way off the stage and we leave the theatre. Here, however, we see the court jester Touchstone embarking on marriage with shameless cynicism, and exploiting it almost as a form of sexual licence. He rejoices in the goatherd Audrey's plainness and rusticity, and welcomes her lack of 'honesty', or chastity, as a promising token of sexual compliance. He wants to be married quickly and casually by a 'hedge-priest', Sir Oliver Martext, 'for he is not like to marry me well; and not being well married, it will be a good excuse for me hereafter to leave my wife' (III.3.82–4). Modern audiences can be shocked by the extent of Touchstone's callousness towards the gullible and low-born Audrey, though a good actor in the part of Touchstone will generally inveigle us into some complicity with it. In any case, Shakespeare's chief interest, as the closing scene suggests, seems to have been in ranking the varieties of marriage on a kind of pyramid, with Touchstone's at the very bottom. Though supposedly instituted to restrain and order sexual desire within a Christian society, marriage itself can be used as a pretext for sexual liberty by those who are unscrupulous enough to do so.

Touchstone's bluntness is all of a piece with the freedom and frankness of speech that is such a pervasive feature of this play. Rosalind, too, is freespoken and down to earth, for instance in her riposte when Celia questions her about her unhappiness, 'But is all this for your father?' 'No, some of it is for my child's father' (I.3.10–11). Some of Shakespeare's earliest editors felt Rosalind's response to be 'indelicate', because of its anticipation of sexual union, conception and childbirth, and emended 'my child's father' to 'my father's child'. Victorian girls were not supposed to imagine themselves too eagerly as wives and mothers, especially with reference to young men whom they hardly knew. Once she is in male disguise Rosalind speaks even more freely. Like Touchstone she is often cynical, as in her celebrated remark that 'men have died from time to time and worms have eaten them, but not for love' (IV.1.96–8), or her merciless put-down to the coquettish Phebe, 'Sell when you can, you are not for all markets' (III.5.60). Though less coarse than Touchstone, she, like him, sees marriage in less than rosy terms: 'men are April when they woo, December when they wed; maids are May when they are maids, but the sky changes when they are wives' (IV.1.136–8). Such bold and unsentimental observations, rather strong meat for the Victorians, have helped to make her the Shakespeare heroine most appealing to modern readers.

In a civilized society freedom of speech is perhaps the greatest of all freedoms. Its importance in the play is stressed most emphatically in the figure of Jaques, the second major character added by Shakespeare to his source in Thomas Lodge's *Rosalynde*. As soon as we hear about him (II.1.26) it is obvious that Jaques is an awkward customer, a social misfit. While the rest of the banished Duke's companions go off to hunt the deer, which provide them with both sport and food, Jaques refuses to join the expedition. But after the event he makes a speech over the mortally wounded stag, whose death is 'moralized' (II.1.44) 'into a thousand similes' (45). His speech over the deer seems at first merely conventional, all of a piece with the sentimentalization of hunted animals and apparent empathy with them that was a regular part of the literature of hunting. However, the climax of Jaques's oration, as reported by the First Lord, is rather less generalized in its 'moralizing', for he uses the image of the wounded stag as pretext for a critique of the Duke's own way of life among his comrades in Arden:

> . . . swearing that we
> Are mere usurpers, tyrants, and what's worse
> To fright the animals and to kill them up
> In their assigned and native dwelling place. (II.1.60–63)

Obliquely accusing the exiled Duke and his companions, victims of usurpation and tyranny, of being themselves both 'usurpers' and 'tyrants' might, one would imagine, get Jaques into trouble with the authorities. Yet on the contrary, the Duke is enchanted by Jaques's perverse ingenuity, and is eager to witness it for himself. Rather than being sidelined, or even punished as a troublemaker and subversive, Jaques enjoys all the privileges of a court favourite. Indeed, the Duke is much fonder of the company of Jaques than Jaques is of that of the Duke: Jaques tries to avoid him. When the Duke at last catches up with Jaques, in Act II, scene 7, the latter uses this meeting to demand yet more freedom of speech, and in particular to ask for freedom to rail without limit against all that he sees as vice and hypocrisy, both in individuals and in society as a whole:

> I must have liberty
> Withal, as large a charter as the wind,
> To blow on whom I please . . . (47–9)

Though the Duke teasingly charges Jaques with having been himself in former times a 'sensual' 'libertine' (66, 65), in practice he not only permits his satirical gibes, but positively encourages him to speak freely. This is made explicit a little later on in the same long scene, when the Duke, moved to pity by Orlando's appeal for sustenance

for the aged Adam, presents Jaques with an explicit cue
for a set-piece speech:

> This wide and universal theatre
> Presents more woeful pageants than the scene
> Wherein we play in. (II.7.138–40)

The Duke's reflection on the stage as a 'universal theatre'
showing 'woeful pageants' (138,139) provokes Jaques's
brilliant account of the seven miserable ages of man
which opens 'All the world's a stage' (140). This is one
of the most frequently quoted passages in Shakespeare's
plays. It has often been taken out of context as if it set
out Shakespeare's own personal summation of the
process of human life from cradle to grave. However,
we must always bear in mind that it is spoken by the
gloomy and cynical Jaques, whose patron positively
encourages his 'sullen fits' (II.1.67). We must also
remember that the narrative context is one of anxiety
and suspense. The dramatic function of the speech is to
divert the attention of the audience, both onstage and
off, while Orlando goes to search for old Adam, who
may, for all we know, be dead. In encouraging Jaques
to speak freely the Duke is not endorsing his bitter view
of life, but rather admiring the ingenuity of rhetoric
with which he expounds it. Both here and later in the
comedy Jaques's ill humour and misanthropy provide
the perfect foil to the Duke's unfailing good humour and
generosity. Earlier in scene 7 Jaques speaks scornfully
and dismissively to Orlando, who has burst in with sword
in hand: 'Of what kind should this cock come of?' (91).
However, the Duke questions the young stranger kindly
and soon establishes his essential 'gentleness' both of
lineage and demeanour. The Duke and Orlando, it

becomes clear, share ideals of piety and social compliance. Implicitly, the nastiness of Jaques is rebuked. His
'All the world's a stage' speech was bitter and negative
(II.7.140). It reduced the course of a man's life to a series
of miseries and frustrations, from the 'mewling and
puking' of infancy to the 'whining' and 'sighing' of
boyhood and young manhood. His account arrives lastly,
by way of middle-aged pomposity, at the sixth and
seventh ages of diminution into 'second childishness',
'Sans teeth, sans eyes, sans taste, sans everything' (167).
However, his depiction of old age in general, and
doddery old men in particular, as pathetic and con-
temptible has been instantly corrected both in actions
and in words. As soon as the speech is over, Orlando
enters carrying the aged and half-starved Adam, to be
greeted by the affable Duke with the line: 'Welcome. Set
down your venerable burden' (168). It's quite clear that
Adam is not to be spurned as a silly old man, but on the
contrary is to be welcomed at the feast as an object of
intense solicitude and affection. In context, the freedom
granted by the Duke to Jaques to rail against and sati-
rize everyone and everything is valuable not so much
because freedom of speech is inherently precious as because the 'sullen' and melancholic vision of life that he
unfolds stimulates all the other characters, and in consequence the play's audience, to arrive at a fuller appreciation of the value of generosity and comradeship.

Though he himself never seems fully to realize this,
Jaques has been set up as a version of the licensed fool.
He is at liberty to speak his mind freely in the presence
of the Duke and his companions, but the price he must
pay for this is that no one will really listen to him or be
persuaded by him, and no one except the Duke will be
truly his friend. Though he delivers many of the most

memorable lines, even in a play exceptionally filled with memorable lines, he is and continues to be essentially an outsider. Four couples come together for marriage in the closing scene, but Jaques prepares for a new kind of withdrawal from society. It seems that it suits him better to be in opposition or self-imposed exile rather than to be associated with active government. Once the banished Duke Senior has been reinstated Jaques is suddenly eager to attach himself to his younger brother Duke Frederick, formerly a usurping tyrant but now a religious convert. Duke and dissident will share an existence as hermits and 'convertites' 'at your abandoned cave' (V.4.181, 193) – possibly originally represented by the middle aperture at the back of the Globe stage – occupying the very same shelter formerly inhabited by Duke Senior. While everyone else will return, reconciled, to the French court, Jaques will continue to find true liberty in exile from society.

'A GREAT RECKONING'

Though it did not reach print until the 1623 first Folio, *As You Like It* is one of the more precisely datable of Shakespeare's plays. It was not included by Francis Meres in his list of Shakespeare's plays in *Palladis Tamia*, written by September 1598. However, it was among four plays, all but one of them by Shakespeare, which were entered in the Stationers' Register on 4 August 1600 in order to block their unlicensed printing. Though *As You Like It* was not printed, the song 'It was a lover and his lass' (V.3.15–38) was included in Thomas Morley's *First Book of Airs* in 1600, and the text there appears to derive from the play. Some external events in 1599–1600 appear to have a bearing on the play's composition. The first and most positive is the opening of the Globe Theatre in Southwark in the late summer of 1599. Whether or not *As You Like It* was actually performed there, there is little doubt that it was planned by Shakespeare as a 'Globe' play. Jaques's lines 'All the world's a stage, | And all the men and women merely players' (II.7.140–41) are both a translation and an expansion of what some scholars believe to have been the motto of the new playhouse, *Totus mundus agit histrionem*. The second significant external event is the 1599 'Bishops' Ban' on satirical and epigrammatic writings. As Cyndia Clegg has argued in her book *Press Censorship in Elizabethan England* (1997), this measure seems to have been chiefly intended to silence criticism of the military expedition to Ireland that summer, led by the Queen's unstable favourite Robert Devereux, Earl of Essex. There are what appear to be two allusions in the play to this major outbreak of state censorship. In Act I, scene 2 Celia speaks of the present moment as the time 'since the little wit that fools have was silenced' (84–5). Many of the works listed by the Bishops were comic, and could therefore be called foolish. And in Act III, scene 3 Touchstone remarks to the dim-witted Audrey that:

> When a man's verses cannot be understood, nor a man's good wit seconded with the forward child Understanding, it strikes a man more dead than a great reckoning in a little room. (10–13)

This has often been read as alluding to the death of Christopher Marlowe, fatally stabbed in a 'little room' in Deptford on 30 May 1593, allegedly because of a quarrel over the 'reckoning', or tavern bill, and probably it does indeed refer to this. *As You Like It* also includes a direct quotation from Marlowe's *Hero and Leander* (printed 1598), preceded by a line paying tribute to him as the 'Dead Shepherd':

> Dead Shepherd, now I find thy saw of might,
> 'Who ever loved, that loved not at first sight?' (III.5.81–2)

(A 'saw' is a saying or aphorism.) Though he had been dead for seven years, there were particular reasons for remembering Marlowe and his poetry in 1599–1600. The books listed by the Bishops to be called in and burned included Marlowe's translation of Ovid's *Elegies*, recently published under a false imprint alongside John Davies's *Epigrams*. An allusion to Marlowe's translations from Ovid in Touchstone's speech is made particularly likely by the fact that his preceding speech concerns 'the most capricious poet, honest Ovid' (III.3.5–6) This suggests a tribute to Ovid (presumably wasted on Audrey), which is combined with a vindication both of his poetry and that of Marlowe as essentially 'honest', in spite of the eroticism of their poetry. Other writers at this time, such as Ben Jonson in *Poetaster* (1600–1601), identified Marlowe with Ovid as a daring poet and playwright who got into trouble with the authorities and was severely punished by them, as Ovid was by the Emperor Augustus.

Later developments in 1599–1600 may have influenced Shakespeare's decision to write a comedy about the pleasures of banishment. These may also have a bearing on the fact that the play did not reach print until 1623. At the end of September 1599 the Earl of Essex, General of the military forces sent to Ireland to suppress the rebellion of the Earl of Tyrone, suddenly returned to England. He had not sought permission from the Queen to relinquish his post, as he was required to do. Nor had he received an adequate submission from the rebel Earl. This impulsive action led quickly to Essex's disgrace and house arrest, with far-reaching consequences. Not only had Essex been a close favourite of the Queen's; he was also a major patron of learning and the arts, and his sphere of influence by the late 1590s was extremely wide. Many writers and scholars looked to him for support and encouragement. He was also the closest friend of the young Earl of Southampton, to whom Shakespeare had dedicated his narrative poems in 1593 and 1594.

Essex's disgrace and the Queen's implacable displeasure had an immediate impact on literature. There was a major explosion of satirical and epigrammatic writing, despite the Bishops' Ban of the preceding summer. His disgrace also caused a major shift of cultural influence away from the court and towards the Essex circle, despite their fall from royal favour. This was a time when a comedy celebrating the pleasures of a greenwood life away from the official seat of government must have seemed to many younger playgoers both attractive and topical.

Indeed, the play may have been too topical for its own good. We have no record of any early performance. And while the other three plays entered in the Stationers' Register in August 1600 quickly reached print, *As You Like It*, as already mentioned, did not. It is possible either that performances of it got the Lord Chamberlain's Men into trouble because of the play's topicality, or that the company themselves decided, as the political crisis of 1600–1601 became more acute, that it would not be prudent either to perform it publicly or to allow it to reach print. It has been suggested that it could have been performed privately at some dissident nobleman's house, such as Essex House in London or Southampton's Hampshire residence, Titchfield. Such a location as Titchfield, in the New Forest, would certainly have suited its subject matter and woodland setting. However, we have no documentary evidence of any such performance. Early allusions are altogether shadowy. For instance, Sir John Harington in 1605 mentioned having fairly recently witnessed a discussion of the ages of man's life 'in the schools'. This could allude to a performance of *As You Like It* in Oxford or Cambridge in which Jaques's 'seven ages' speech was the most memorable scene (partly because of its famous speech), as it has been in many modern productions. But it may just as well refer to an academic debate, since the ages and stages of human life had been much discussed since the Middle Ages.

The theme of man's ages, and especially of the last two phases of decrepitude, was a good deal more topical and risky than modern readers may realize. The Queen was now in her late sixties, and the myth of her agelessness and enduring beauty was being taken to new extremes by playwrights and poets. In the Epilogue to his comedy *Old Fortunatus*, performed at court in 1599–1600, Thomas Dekker showed two old men praying that when their grandsons are themselves old men Elizabeth may still be alive and on the throne. Indeed, they pray for her reign to extend for another four hundred years, which would bring her almost to today. They also desire defeat to 'those that wish thee harm' – presumably an allusion to Tyrone's rebellion in Ireland. The rhetoric of loyalty could hardly be more fulsome. In the same year Sir John Davies, in his *Hymnes of Astraea*, praised the sixty-eight-year-old Elizabeth as both 'Queen of beauty' and an embodiment of eternal spring. To

draw attention, at such a time, to the universality of the
ageing process was in effect treasonous. The Lord
Chamberlain's Men, some of whose plays were regularly
chosen for performance at court during the Christmas
holidays, may have realized that Jaques's unsparing
account of extreme old age as 'second childishness and
mere oblivion' ruled out court performance of *As You
Like It*, despite the fact, already discussed, that Jaques's
satirical account of the last two ages is immediately coun-
teracted by the benevolent treatment of old Adam.

There was another literary work of the period
1599–1600 that discussed the 'ages of man', and this one
was definitely linked with resentment of Elizabeth's long-
drawn-out regime. A treatise called 'The difference of
the ages of mans life' was written by the secretary and
evil genius of the Earl of Essex, the Oxford academic
Henry Cuffe. Though much of Cuffe's treatise concerns
variations in lifespan, he also discusses the traditional
'ages of man' first schematized by Aristotle. He offers
almost as unflattering a picture as Jaques does of the
'last Scene of all', which supposedly sets in after the age
of sixty-five:

... which we call decrepit old age ... when our strength and
heat is so far decayed, that not only all ability is taken away,
but even willingness ... Decrepit old age, from the angry
aspect of dry Saturn, sucketh the poisonous infirmities of crazy
sickness and wayward pettiness.

Cuffe's treatise did not reach print until 1607, by which
time Elizabeth was safely dead. But it bore the date '1600'
on its title page, thus drawing attention to the precise time
of its composition, a year during which many younger
courtiers became increasingly restless and impatient with

the regime of a childless woman, who had now reached the 'last Scene of all', 'decrepit old age'. It was Cuffe who was held chiefly responsible for egging on Essex and Southampton to their 'rising', or attempted coup, in the City of London on 8 February 1601. Essex was executed in the Tower, and his close associate Henry Cuffe, not being a nobleman, was hanged at Tyburn. All in all, Shakespeare and his company got off rather lightly during this difficult period, perhaps because they were prudent enough to keep *As You Like It* under wraps. None of them had to pay the 'great reckoning' of a second death – censorship and suppression – that had been endured by the already-dead Christopher Marlowe.

'LOVE'S PRICK AND ROSALIND'

Although *As You Like It* may have made little impact on Shakespeare's contemporaries, being rarely performed, if at all, in the early seventeenth century and never printed in Shakespeare's lifetime, it was eventually to become one of his best-loved comedies. For many later generations its discussions of tyranny, the ageing process and the need for free speech have not seemed particularly important. From the mid eighteenth century onwards it has been enjoyed chiefly as a playful comedy about love and good fellowship, full of memorable set-piece speeches, good jokes, and piquant love scenes. It has the added bonus of showing an attractive woman dressed as an equally attractive young man. Even to modern audiences, for whom neither pastoral romance nor courtly love poetry are familiar genres, it has been obvious that it also has enjoyable elements of send-up and burlesque. The conventions of love melancholy, and of the wooing of an obdurate lady by a poetically gifted young man, are vividly acted out, yet at the same time mercilessly ridiculed. Though most audiences will be inclined to view Orlando, for instance, as a true lover, his true love inspires him to compose some appallingly bad verses. Read aloud by Touchstone and Rosalind in Act III, scene 2, these doggerel rhymes are both absurd and – accidentally? – bawdy, in a way that undercuts their sentimentality: 'He that sweetest rose will find, | Must find love's prick and Rosalind' (107–8). Yet we think none the worse of Orlando for being such a bad poet. Phebe, too, descends to doggerel when she falls passionately in love with 'Ganymede' in Act III, scene 5. Lightly and deftly Shakespeare pulls the rug from beneath the whole tradition of courtly love poetry that originated with poets such as Petrarch, and implied that the intensity of a lover's passion could be accurately gauged through the ingenuity of his writing. On the strained conventions of love poetry, as on those of romantic marriage, the play breathes agreeably modern-seeming fresh air. While incorporating more songs and poems than any other play by Shakespeare, even *Love's Labour's Lost*, *As You Like It* mocks the pretensions of poets and lyricists.

Shakespeare may also have set out specifically to parody and ridicule his source, Thomas Lodge's *Rosalynde*. This romance, written in the ornate style of Lyly's *Euphues* (1578), was very popular. It went through at least four editions from 1590 to 1598. Very few copies survive from these early print runs, suggesting that some other editions may have been read out of existence. Like Shakespeare's play, *Rosalynde* is full of poems and songs – twenty-one in all. None of the songs in the play is directly based on or cribbed from any of those in

Rosalynde. But Orlando's verses in Act III, scene 2, with their repeated rhyme on 'Rosalind', may owe something to the poetic description of Rosalynde by Rosader, the equivalent of Orlando, which has the clumsy refrain:

> Heigh ho, fair Rosalynde . . .
> Heigh ho, would she were mine.

The slightly comic 'Heigh ho', which represents a sigh, is echoed and repeated by Shakespeare in the song sung by Amiens in Act II, scene 7, with its refrain beginning:

> Hey-ho, sing hey-ho, unto the green holly.

Rosader's next song also closely resembles the doggerel rhymes of Shakespeare's Orlando:

> . . . when as I talk of Rosalynde,
> The god from kindness waxeth kind,
> And seems in self-same flames to fry
> Because he loves as well as I.

Compare Orlando's verses in *As You Like It*, beginning:

> *From the east to western Ind,*
> *No jewel is like Rosalind.*
> *Her worth being mounted on the wind*
> *Through all the world bears Rosalind* . . . (III.2.84–7)

These lines are quickly parodied by Touchstone in the verses beginning:

> If a hart do lack a hind,
> Let him seek out Rosalind . . . (97–8)

Although Lodge, unlike Shakespeare, does not appear to be ridiculing the poetic efforts of his characters, only a little further exaggeration of their already exaggerated style was required to make such verses appear exquisitely absurd.

Shakespeare's heroine Rosalind is quite closely based on Lodge's Rosalynde. Each girl, banished by the usurping monarch who has already banished her father, flees to the Forest of Arden disguised as 'Ganymede'. The equivalent of Shakespeare's Celia is Lodge's Alinda, who changes her name, as Celia does, to Aliena. A further name change has a brilliant simplicity. The faithful old family servant, who in *Rosalynde* is called Adam Spencer — a 'spencer' was a steward — is reduced to plain 'Adam'. This enables Shakespeare to suggest that he embodies our common humanity, being both archetypally 'humane' and symbolically deserving of fellow-feeling. The equivalent of Orlando, as mentioned, is Rosader — a name which is confusingly similar to Rosalind, and could have caused confusion when speech-prefixes were written in abbreviated form in a prompt-book or actor's 'part'. In selecting the name 'Orlando', Shakespeare was making a playful allusion to a more famous Orlando, the crusading hero of Ariosto's long verse romance *Orlando Furioso*. This was translated from the original Italian by Sir John Harington and published in 1591 by Shakespeare's Stratford schoolfellow Richard Field. But while Ariosto's Orlando is driven mad by jealous love, under whose influence he pulls up trees by the roots and dismembers peasants, Shakespeare's Orlando is a gentle, good-natured young man who, far from being mad, is teased by Rosalind for *not* being mad. While melancholy lovers should supposedly be distracted and careless in dress and demeanour, 'you are rather point-device in your accoutrements, as loving yourself, than seeming the lover of any other' (III.2.366–8). *Orlando Furioso* may have been fresh in the minds of theatregoers because of a revival of interest in Robert Greene's fairly simplistic play on the theme, reprinted in 1599, in which Orlando is shown both as going mad and as writing poetry. Shakespeare also turned to *Orlando Furioso* for the name of Orlando's elder brother Oliver, whose equivalent in *Rosalynde* is Saladyne.

While Shakespeare made many subtle changes to Lodge's *Rosalynde*, he followed its outlines quite closely. He retained the essentials of its plot, and seems even to have drawn on the book for his title. In his dedicatory epistle '*To the Gentlemen Readers*' Lodge includes the phrase 'If you like it; so'. But he softened the more violent elements of the romance. In *Rosalynde* a Norman wrestler breaks the necks of two young opponents, killing them in full view of their heartbroken father, while in *As You Like It* Charles the Wrestler merely stuns them and cracks their ribs (I.2). *Rosalynde* closes with a pitched battle in which the usurping Duke Torismond, the original of Duke Frederick, is killed. In Shakespeare Duke Frederick is deflected from bloodthirsty military ambitions by a timely encounter with 'an old religious man' (V.4.156–62). However, though less violent, *As You Like It* faithfully reflects the spirit of the central parts of *Rosalynde*, which are playful, leisurely and full not only of poems, songs and verse dialogues but also of enjoyable set speeches. Lodge's leisurely and often somewhat diffuse pastoral is cleverly mirrored in a comedy whose central scenes feel extremely leisurely, yet do not take all that long to perform. In Act III, scene 2, for instance, Rosalind and Orlando – who claims 'there's no clock in the forest' (292–3) though Touchstone apparently has a pocket sundial – engage in a very leisurely discussion of the nature of time, and of the ways in which it 'travels in divers paces with divers persons' (299–300). The illusory pace at which time appears to move is both a theme of the play and a feature of its construction. Shakespeare exploits our subjective experience of time in the theatre. While we are caught up in enjoyment of the play there appears to be all the time in the world. But we may be astonished, once the play is over, to find that it took no more than a couple of hours. *As You Like It* is in truth one of Shakespeare's shorter plays, though it can be made to take up more or less time in performance according to the elaboration or otherwise of the performance of the songs and of such spectacles as the entry of Hymen in Act V, scene 4.

One of two major ways in which Shakespeare's play diverges from Lodge's romance is in didacticism. The framework of *Rosalynde* is insistently moral. At the beginning Sir John of Bordeaux, the equivalent of 'old Sir Rowland', bequeaths a store of good advice and admonition to his three sons, and particularly warns them against falling in love: 'Fancy is a fickle thing, and beauty's paintings are tricked up with time's colours, which being set to dry in the sun, perish with the same.' The inherent misogyny of this admonition, which implies that women's beauty is both specious and worthless, is quite foreign to the tone of Shakespeare's play. The ending of Lodge's romance is even more insistently didactic, as the narrator observes that the story has shown

that virtue is not measured by birth but by action, that younger brethren though inferior in years may be superior to honours, that concord is the sweetest conclusion, and amity betwixt brothers more forceable than fortune.

While Hymen's song in the final scene of *As You Like
It* celebrates social 'concord' –

> Then is there mirth in heaven,
> When earthly things, made even,
>   Atone together. (105–7)

– there is no sense that the audience are being belaboured
with any particular admonition or moral. Indeed, some
of the play's earliest critics felt it to be worryingly deficient in moral teaching. In his edition of Shakespeare
(1765) Samuel Johnson found its plot 'wild and pleasing',
and praised the 'heroism' of Celia's friendship with
Rosalind. He complained, however, that:

By hastening to the end of his work Shakespeare suppressed
the dialogue between the usurper and the hermit, and lost an
opportunity of exhibiting a moral lesson in which he might
have found matter worthy of his powers. (*Johnson on
Shakespeare* (ed. Arthur Sherbo, 1968), vol. vii)

Perhaps Johnson would have preferred Lodge's romance,
had he known it. Yet Shakespeare must have made a
deliberate decision – as he normally did when adapting
source material – to exclude the didactic conclusions of
the original in favour of crowd-pleasing merriment. In
place of Lodge's checklist of moral lessons he gave his
audience the Epilogue, in which the boy actor playing
Rosalind, presumably still dressed in bridal array, flirts
with them outrageously, while also urging them to flirt
(to put it mildly) with each other:

> I charge you, O women, for the love you bear to men, to
> like as much of this play as please you; and I charge you,

> O men, for the love you bear to women – as I perceive by
> your simpering, none of you hates them – that between
> you and the women the play may please. (V.4.206–11)

The comedy that the audience has just enjoyed mutates,
in a bawdy slippage worthy of Touchstone, into the
sexual 'play' with which audience members may
shortly pleasure each other. None of Shakespeare's comedies, even the most festive, ends with a more overt
endorsement of sexual gratification. This is also the only
play of Shakespeare's in which the 'lady' delivers the
Epilogue. In early performances, with Rosalind played
by a talented boy actor, it would have offered a complex
conjunction of 'love's prick and Rosalind' (III.2.108),
since the actor dressed as a bride was nevertheless
equipped with a real 'prick', or penis. It seems not so
much that gender distinctions are confused as that
gender boundaries have been elided, aptly rounding off
a play that celebrates every kind of freedom, as its very
title suggests.

'THIS IS THE FOREST OF ARDEN'

The other major way in which Shakespeare's play
diverges from its source is in its treatment of place.
Lodge's Forest of Arden is emphatically Mediterranean,
with hot sun and groves of oranges and lemons. Many
details remind readers that the tale is set in France. For
instance, when he dresses up for the joint nuptials,
Coridon – the equivalent of Shakespeare's Corin – puts
on a green hat 'whereon stood a copper brooch with the
picture of Saint Denis', Denis being the patron saint of
France. Some well-read readers of *Rosalynde* may also

have noticed that a large number of its songs and poems
are translated from two contemporary French poets,
Ronsard and Desportes. In Shakespeare's play, however,
the setting becomes increasingly fluid and indeterminate,
itself partaking of the freedom that is the play's theme.
The opening scenes at court are distinctly French in
perspective. Charles the Wrestler alludes to the banished
Duke living 'in the Forest of Arden, and a many merry
men with him; and there they live like the old Robin
Hood of England' (I.1.108–10) – thus drawing attention
to his own location in France and not England. Orlando,
who challenges Charles to a wrestling match, is called
'the stubbornest young fellow of France' (132–3). The
Duke's servant Monsieur le Beau is French in both his
title and his name. It is true that Duke Senior also has
some companions with French names, such as the musical
Amiens and the satirical Jaques. It is also true that the
farm purchased by Celia and Rosalind is located by a
'tuft of olives' (III.5.75). But both landscape and location, once everyone is well settled in Arden, seem increasingly fantastic and exotic. Rosalind claims to have found
Orlando's verses hanging on 'a palm-tree' (III.2.170–71),
for instance. And when Oliver asks the way to
'Ganymede's' farm, 'A sheepcote fenced about with olive
trees' (IV.3.78), Celia's instructions are both confused
and confusing:

> West of this place, down in the neighbour bottom,
> The rank of osiers by the murmuring stream
> Left on your right hand brings you to the place. (79–81)

Though editors have rationalized 'Left on your right
hand' as 'leaving behind the rank of osiers on your right
hand', in the theatre the line is far more likely to be heard

by the audience as a nonsensical direction that will raise a laugh. The absurdity of Celia's directions reaches its climax when she explains that there is in any case no point in Oliver going there, since the house is empty. The proximity of olive trees to Rosalind and Celia's farmhouse turns out to be just one exotic detail in a fanciful description of a pastoral nowhere.

Arden is a place where sheep graze and goats nibble, and yet characters may equally well encounter suckling lionesses and green and gold snakes. There is much talk of bad weather from new arrivals – bitter winds, rain and snow – yet at no point does any character appear to be in the least inconvenienced by its climatic conditions. In so far as we have any sense of specific location in Acts II–V, it feels much more like England than France. The name 'Arden' is a kind of geographical pun, for in addition to forests of Arden or Ardennes in Belgium and France, England had its very own Forest of Arden. This also happened to be the area within which Shakespeare was born, a personal association reinforced by 'Arden' being his mother's maiden name. This great forest once extended across a wide band of Middle England, as far as the River Trent in the north and the River Severn in the south. The word 'forest' did not necessarily denote continuous woodland, but could designate a large predominantly wooded area with many clearings and small areas of cultivation. The Forest of Arden was already much diminished by the later Middle Ages, yet fragments of it survived, and still survive, in some woodlands close to Stratford, such as Bannam Wood near Henley-in-Arden and Withycombe Wood near Stratford. Whether or not a modern audience is aware of all this, the name will still tend to have an 'English' resonance. Many of the play's social and cultural references also seem English. The court Clown is Master Touchstone, not Monsieur Touchstone, and his account of how he wooed the rustic milkmaid Jane Smile and kissed 'the cow's dugs that her pretty chopt hands had milked' (II.4.45–6) sounds entirely English because of Jane Smile's name, the homely word 'dugs' and the word 'chopt' (or 'chapped'), which suggests exposure to raw English weather. And though there are of course churches and gentlemen's houses in France as well as in England, Orlando's reminiscence of the 'better days' once enjoyed by himself and the Duke also comes across as an idealized account of provincial England:

> If ever you have looked on better days;
> If ever been where bells have knolled to church;
> If ever sat at any good man's feast;
> If ever from your eyelids wiped a tear,
> And know what 'tis to pity and be pitied ... (II. 7.114–18)

Like his eulogy of the faithful Adam for his embodiment of 'the constant service of the antique world' (II.3.57), Orlando's speech to the Duke alludes to the powerful myth of Merrie England, a place of unbounded generosity and good fellowship best known from the folklore tales of Robin Hood.

As well as suggesting Merrie England, the Forest of Arden also alludes, self-referentially, to the stage. Not for nothing does the Duke describe his forest court as 'This wide and universal theatre' (II.7.138). The trees on which Orlando has hung his verses may have been originally represented neither by stage palm trees nor by stage fruit trees, but simply by the wooden pillars that supported the upper stage in the Globe Theatre. Like the theatre itself – the Globe or any theatre – the Forest of Arden is a place where extraordinary things are done and spoken, and extraordinary people keep turning up, yet no one is really surprised.

Minor characters are apt to appear from nowhere, speak very few lines, and then vanish again as abruptly as they entered. Many of these minor roles can be performed by a single actor. A sense of 'not him again!' can reduce an audience to helpless mirth if they see the same performer appearing (say) as Sir Oliver Martext, the hedge-priest in Act III, scene 3, as Audrey's rustic suitor William in Act V, scene 1, and finally as '*Second Brother, Jaques de Boys*' in the closing moments of Act V, scene 4. None of these minor figures is strictly speaking essential to the plot. Martext and William appear onstage chiefly as hapless butts for Touchstone's raillery, and he sends them off again with brutal finality. William often raises a laugh with his touchingly good-humoured farewell to his rival Touchstone, 'God rest you merry, sir' (V.1.58). Jaques de Boys gives an account of Duke Frederick's sudden conversion which could just as well have been reported by someone else. It has sometimes been suggested that the play's profusion of minor char-acters, together with their tendency to share names either with other characters or with the author himself, is the result of carelessness by a playwright composing at speed. We encounter a major and a minor Jaques, a major and a minor Oliver, and even a name held by the poet himself, William Shakespeare, here assigned modestly to the bumpkin William. Given the topicality of its theme, the play may indeed have been written at speed. Yet it is actually well constructed, with no major discrepancies or loose ends. It is a good deal more water-tight, as a narrative, than *Much Ado About Nothing*, written a year or two earlier. Like so much else in the play,

Shakespeare's inclusion of a second character called Oliver, a second Jaques and a provincial rustic called William are probably all deliberate jokes and absurdities.

Comic genre does not necessarily guarantee that a play will be designed to offer a lot of laughs. The bottom line for the definition of comedy is not that there will be continuous humour but that none of the characters will die and lovers will get married. Some of Shakespeare's later comedies, such as *The Merchant of Venice*, restrict their explicit humour to a few scenes. But this comedy, with its two entertaining jesters, Jaques and Touchstone, together with a cross-dressed heroine who, by means both of actions and speech, can generate even more laughter than they do, has unusually high entertainment value throughout, at least from Act II onwards. It incorporates comic dialogue and quickfire repartee, stand-up comic monologues such as Touchstone's account of the 'lie seven times removed' in the final scene, and many verbal jokes and plays of fancy which are woven into the fabric of the text. The Forest of Arden is not merely a refuge from oppression but a place of relaxed pleasure, generous friendship and an abundance of therapeutic laughter, both onstage and off. This makes *As You Like It*, more than any other play by Shakespeare, an explicit celebration of theatre itself. Just as refugees from tyranny can discover freedom and healing in the forest, stressed or depressed playgoers can discover freedom and healing in the theatre. This is as true today as it was in 1600.

Katherine Duncan-Jones

The Play in Performance

Although *As You Like It* may have been specifically written for performance at the Globe Theatre in or around 1600, we have no definite record to prove it was ever seen there. It also seems likely that it was performed by the King's Men at the small indoor Blackfriars Theatre during the Stuart period, since the company undoubtedly possessed the text of the play. But here again there is no evidence of any specific performance. Rather tellingly, the earliest firm record we have is of a heavily adapted version made by Charles Johnson, which was performed at the Drury Lane Theatre in 1723. The Prologue to Johnson's *Love in a Forest*, which offers to 'give the stage from Shakespeare one play more', suggests that the comedy may have been unfamiliar to audiences of the time. Johnson's play was cobbled together with additions from several other plays, including *Richard II*. It retained the main narrative outlines, but Touchstone was omitted, along with half a dozen other characters. With its exceptionally high incidence of poems, set speeches and songs, together with an exciting wrestling match and a closing dance, *As You Like It* seems always to have attracted adaptation. It is relatively easy to add or subtract episodes, since it already falls into various and varied segments.

As early as 1741 the play was also converted into an opera, or at least into a succession of Handel-like arias, by the Italian composer Francesco Veracini. However, neither Johnson's adaptation nor Veracini's opera was especially popular. Veracini's opera achieved ten performances at Drury Lane, Johnson's play only five. As we shall see, there seems to be a consistent tendency for strongly adapted versions of the play to do less well than more faithful treatments. Yet adaptations, especially musical ones, continue to be made. Three recent examples are Niels Cary Engleberg's rock musical score (1969), John R. Briggs's musical *Phalstaffs Phollies* (1977) and Peter Spelmann's country and western version *Tanglin' Hearts* (1981).

The stage history of the play proper began in 1740, when it was performed at the Drury Lane Theatre in London with Hannah Pritchard (1709–68), now better remembered for her Lady Macbeth, as Rosalind. This was such a success that the play was soon also staged at the rival Covent Garden Theatre, and at one point was being played at both theatres simultaneously. From 1741 the Drury Lane's Rosalind was Peg Woffington (?1720–60), who continued in this role for many years, until in 1757 she suffered an incapacitating stroke onstage while she was halfway through her delivery of the Epilogue. The major role of Rosalind, the longest and theatrically most rewarding female role in the whole of Shakespeare's works, may have been the key to the comedy's huge popularity during a period when the stage was dominated by great actresses. Rosalind's disguise as the man or boy 'Ganymede' had the additional advantage of catering for the eighteenth-century fashion for actresses to show off their legs in 'breeches' roles. Peg Woffington so much enjoyed playing 'breeches' parts that she also appropriated a few 'straight' male roles in other plays of the period. Even Sarah Siddons, though much more celebrated for her Lady Macbeth, also played Rosalind, first in the provinces early in her career, and later in London in 1785 and 1786. Increasing age seems to have been no handicap for the great Rosalinds of the day. Mrs Spranger Barry played the part every year from 1766 to 1778, by which time she was forty-four.

From the mid eighteenth century until today the play has rarely been out of the English repertoire for more than a year or two. *As You Like It*, and especially Rosalind, continued to be extremely popular throughout the nineteenth century, both in England and beyond. Celebrated Victorian Rosalinds included the swashbuckling Mrs Nesbitt and the more subtle and tender Helen Faucit. The American actress Mary Anderson played the role in 1885, and Ada Rehan played Rosalind in New York, London and Paris in 1889–90. Because of the importance of location in the play, it also offers scope for extremely lavish sets, a potential that was fully exploited in W. C. Macready's lavish production at Drury Lane in 1842, which included a vast medieval French chateau for Duke Frederick's court. This also made the play an appealing Shakespeare text in the early days of cinema. Silent films based on it were made as early as 1908, 1912 (twice) and 1915. However, it has not been filmed particularly often in modern times, relative to other Shakespeare comedies. The films most readily available on video are Basil Coleman's 1978 BBC version and Christine Edzard's film of 1992.

As You Like It was one of the first three plays to be performed at the Shakespeare Festival in Toronto, Canada, in 1949. By the 1950s it was enjoying productions all over the world, including Eastern Europe, then largely communist, and Australia. The possibility of

presenting the tyrannical rule of Duke Frederick's court
as either a fascist or a communist dictatorship led to a
spate of politicized interpretations of the play from the
early 1970s onwards. In many of these Jaques was shown
either as an outsider, a political dissident or a student
agitator. John Caird's RSC production in 1989 alluded
to the recent collapse of communist regimes in Eastern
Europe, showing Duke Frederick's court as a monument
of oppressive totalitarian architecture, which had to be
painfully dismantled by the dissident exiles to reveal the
forest floor below. This production also literalized the
Forest of Arden's 'winter and rough weather', showing
the refugees making their escape through blizzards. Even
in Arden they wore heavy greatcoats and huddled
together for warmth, which somewhat hampered the
expressiveness of their gestures and movement.

In recent years the play has lent itself surprisingly
well to further topical allusions, such as the major foot-
and-mouth epidemic that crippled British farming in the
year 2000, the increasing political strength of the conser-
vative and pro-hunting Countryside Alliance, and wider-
ranging concerns with ecology and the environment.
Latterly, most British productions have given *As You
Like It* some sort of topical spin. This has led to a strong
emphasis on visual effect and/or deeper meaning, sometimes to the detriment of both individual performances
and overall comic effect. 'Topical' treatments, of one
kind or another, have tended to suffer from low entertainment value. Modern design-driven interpretation
reached its apogee in 2000. Gregory Doran's RSC
production was designed by Kaffe Fasset, better known
as a brilliant designer of colourful knitwear and tapestry.
Rosalind was shown in Act I working on a tapestry
picture, which perhaps symbolized her dream of pastoral

freedom. The contrast between court and forest was shown as a transition from elegant black-and-white patterned Renaissance costumes to richly coloured knitting and textiles. As Michael Dobson exclaimed in *Shakespeare Survey 54* (2001):

Those rose-embroidered cushions! That green-tapestry-hills stagecloth! Corin's hat! The Ganymede earth-tones pullover! Celia's sleeves! The flower-embroidered gauze that fell for Hymen's entrance in Act 5! – there was a real visual wit to this design, which it would have been churlish not to enjoy.

Despite the production's emphasis on visual design, little theatrical capital was made of Rosalind's disguise as a boy, or man. Her costume change suggested that rather than changing gender she had made a journey through time from the oppressive hierarchies of Renaissance courts to the laid-back manners of young people in the 1970s, sporting a unisex woolly jumper that was beautifully designed but theatrically inert. Because there was little sense of her performing masculinity, the comic potential of her proxy-wooing of Orlando was largely wasted.

More recently, Gregory Thompson's production at Stratford's Swan Theatre (2003) framed the play with additions at the beginning and end. The performance opened with an extended wordless sequence in which Orlando wearily chopped wood, and it closed – on the press night in Stratford but never thereafter – with a coda in which first Duke Frederick and Jaques, and eventually the whole cast, slowly intoned the hymn 'The Lord's my Shepherd'. Programme notes indicated that the audience were supposed to think about the miseries suffered by agricultural labourers in early modern

England, while also having green thoughts about something essentially 'holy' inherent in the natural environment. However, the central position given to the theme of religious conversion unbalanced the text, in which the conversions of Duke Frederick and Jaques work chiefly as a device to dispose of loose ends in the narrative.

The most popular modern productions have been ones that have focused on more obvious themes in the text, in particular its interest in gender and in various types of love relationship. As far as gender goes, as early as 1893–4 the play was performed in New York by an all-female cast, some wearing false beards. A London production with an all-female cast immediately followed. Surprisingly, however, given the rise of feminism during this period, all-female casts were not much of a feature of twentieth-century productions. All-male casts, on the other hand, were widespread in the last quarter century, and some of these were quite celebrated. Clifford Williams's all-male production for the National Theatre in 1967 starred Ronald Pickup as a highbrow Rosalind and Charles Kay as a bespectacled Celia. Though this was stylish and ground-breaking, it was seen by many critics as gimmicky, and was implicitly corrected by David Jones's RSC production the following year, which starred Janet Suzman as a beatnik Rosalind. It should be remembered that in 1967 homosexual acts between consenting adult males had only just been decriminalized. Audience acceptance of homoerotic love scenes still had a long way to go. Only in the last decade of the twentieth century was the play's full homoerotic potential developed. The landmark all-male production was Declan Donellan's for the Cheek by Jowl touring company in 1991. This also featured two excellent black actors, Adrian Lester as an emotionally complex Rosalind and Joe Dixon as a gay Jaques. At the turn of the century audiences have become more sophisticated and flexible in their response to cross-gender casting, which sometimes, yet by no means always, carries homoerotic resonances.

As for love relationships, our interest can be engaged in the central relationship with a wide range of treatments of Rosalind. Some female Rosalinds have not looked in the least like boys, which has had the effect of making Orlando seem particularly love-blind in failing to penetrate her disguise. An example was Samantha Bond's charmingly feminine and bosomy RSC Rosalind/Ganymede in 1992. Other Rosalinds, whether played by men or women, have been more convincingly masculine in costume and physique, such as Eileen Atkins's slender denim-clad version in 1973 (RSC). This can work very well, too. But however Rosalind is played, it is always clear that hers must be the leading role, while that of Orlando is relatively unimportant. The essential requirement is not so much that Orlando's performance matches up to Rosalind's as that the audience are convinced that the couple really and truly are passionately attracted to each other. In this respect the play resembles *Romeo and Juliet*, where again the part of the heroine is both longer and more complex than that of the hero, but it is essential that the audience believe in their mutual passion. In *As You Like It*, as already mentioned, it is not uncommon for the naively adoring Silvius to upstage the more sophisticated Orlando. The apparently secondary romantic role of Silvius has been played by several actors who have gone on to great things, such as Greg Hicks, who played the role at the National in 1979, and Joseph Fiennes, who played it for the RSC in 1992.

Indeed, it is an attractive feature of *As You Like It* in performance that all of its supporting roles are so well individualized. Both Touchstone and Jaques, the two jester figures that Shakespeare added to his source, offer tremendous scope for interpretation and display, with their passages of repartee and monologue. There is also plenty of scope for the addition of physical humour. It's telling that Kenneth Branagh chose to play Touchstone rather than Orlando in his rumbustious Renaissance Theatre Company production at the Phoenix Theatre in London in 1988. The female supporting roles can also be rewarding, and may also benefit from powerful casting. Margaret Drabble, now celebrated as a novelist rather than an actress, played Audrey for the RSC in 1961. Fiona Shaw played Celia for the RSC in 1985. Even the many tiny, apparently supernumerary roles (see p. xlix) offer a young performer some opportunities to make a lasting impression on an audience. However, the large number of actors required for a full performance, even with a good deal of doubling, may be among the reasons why the play has not been performed quite so often as it deserves. It also requires music and singing. Though a cast may get away with performing some of the songs a bit clumsily, the text will not permit this in every case. More positively, a production can be made particularly delightful with the support of first-class singing (see The Songs).

Katherine Duncan-Jones

Further Reading

Agnes Latham's Arden edition (1975) continues to be valuable, and is especially informative on Shakespeare's handling of the source and on the play's likely date and context. Meanwhile, two recent editions are a good deal more illuminating than is the Arden on matters such as performance history and staging. Alan Brissenden's Oxford text (1993) is first-rate in every way, and especially helpful on music, spectacle and dance. Michael Hattaway's introduction to his New Cambridge edition (2000) incorporates useful and original discussions of 'Theatrical genre', 'Pastoral' and 'Counter-pastoral'. It also includes, as do most editions, some well-chosen extracts from Thomas Lodge's *Rosalynde* (here *Rosalind*). A full modernized text of Lodge's romance was edited by Donald Beecher in 1997. However, the fullest discussion of Shakespeare's handling of his sources, and the best text, continues to be that included in Geoffrey Bullough's *Narrative and Dramatic Sources of Shakespeare* (vol. II, 1958).

Some of the historical background to two matters discussed in the Introduction, the 1599 'Bishops' Ban' on satirical works and the rise and fall of the Earl of Essex, can be studied in Cyndia Clegg, *Press Censorship in Elizabethan England* (1997) and Paul Hammer, *The*

Polarisation of Elizabethan Politics: The Political Career of Robert Devereux, 2nd Earl of Essex, 1598–1597 (1999). Another topic discussed in the Introduction is attitudes to old age, of which the classic study is Keith Thomas, 'Age and Authority in Early Modern England', *Proceedings of the British Academy* LXII (1977), pp. 205–48. For both traditional and developing theories of the 'ages of man', see J. A. Burrow, *The Ages of Man: A Study in Medieval Writing and Thought* (1986). On the cult of the Queen, see Helen Hackett, *Virgin Mother, Maiden Queen: Elizabeth I and the cult of the Virgin Mary* (1995; pbk 1996). Enid Welsford, *The Fool: His Social and Literary History* (1935) continues to be the fullest historical study of the varieties of licensed fool. Samuel Johnson's comments on the play can be read in H. R. Woudhuysen, *Johnson on Shakespeare* (1989).

Critical debate about *As You Like It* has focused chiefly on the extent to which it can, or cannot, be called a 'happy comedy', festive and escapist. While John Russell Brown (*Shakespeare and His Comedies* (1962)) and Ruth Nevo (*Comic Transformations in Shakespeare* (1980)) both find the play to be essentially happy, and this has been the traditional view, some more recent critics have stressed the importance of its darker elements. These include such obvious ones as the bitter railing of Jaques, as well as less conspicuous ones such as the passing suggestions that rural life is harsh and oppressive, as indicated in Corin's account of his 'churlish' master (II.4.75–9). The reinstatement of conventional hierarchies, both social and political, which used to be viewed as normative and festive, has more recently been seen as disquieting. Peter Erickson, for instance, finds the play to reinforce a tyrannical social order, and especially male dominance over women (*Patriarchal Structures in*

Shakespeare's Drama (1985)). A similar approach is adopted by Marilyn L. Williamson in *The Patriarchy of Shakespeare's Comedies* (1986). Homoerotic strands in the play are analysed by Valerie Traub in her *Desire and Anxiety: Circulations of Sexuality in Shakespearean Drama* (1992). Another useful study of gender and performance is Stephen Orgel's *Impersonations* (1996).

As a starting point, many students may want to examine the play broadly in the context of Shakespeare's comedies. Two collections provide excellent critical introductions. Emma Smith's *Shakespeare's Comedies* (2003) is a lucid and helpful introduction to five key topics: genre, historical context, gender, language and performance. Slightly more advanced is Richard Dutton and Jean Howard's *Companion to Shakespeare's Works: Volume III: The Comedies* (2003), in which the chapter on *As You Like It* is written by Juliet Dusinberre.

Useful summaries of productions of the play, year by year, are to be found in the annual *Shakespeare Survey*. For Michael Dobson's witty account of 2000, 'the Year of *As You Like It*', see *Shakespeare Survey 54* (2001), pp. 265–74.

AS YOU LIKE IT

The Characters in the Play

DUKE Senior, a banished duke

AMIENS \
JAQUES } noblemen in attendance on him

DUKE Frederick, his brother, the usurper

LE BEAU, a courtier

CHARLES, a wrestler

OLIVER \
JAQUES } sons of Sir Rowland de Boys
ORLANDO /

ADAM \
DENNIS } servants of Oliver

The clown, alias TOUCHSTONE

SIR OLIVER Martext, a country vicar

CORIN \
SILVIUS } shepherds

WILLIAM, a country youth, in love with Audrey

ROSALIND, daughter of Duke Senior, later disguised as
Ganymede

CELIA, daughter of Duke Frederick, later disguised as
Aliena

PHEBE, a shepherdess
AUDREY, a country wench

A masquer representing HYMEN

LORDS, PAGES, and attendants

ORLANDO As I remember, Adam, it was upon this fashion bequeathed me by will, but poor a thousand crowns, and, as thou sayest, charged my brother on his blessing to breed me well; and there begins my sadness. My brother Jaques he keeps at school, and report speaks goldenly of his profit: for my part, he keeps me rustically at home, or, to speak more properly, stays me here at home unkept – for call you that 'keeping' for a gentleman of my birth, that differs not from the stalling of an ox? His horses are bred better, for, besides that they are fair with their feeding, they are taught their manage, and to that end riders dearly hired; but I, his brother, gain nothing under him but growth, for the which his animals on his dunghills are as much bound to him as I. Besides this nothing that he so plentifully gives me, the something that nature gave me his countenance seems to take from me: he lets me feed with his hinds, bars me the place of a brother, and, as much as in him lies, mines my gentility with my education. This is it, Adam, that grieves me, and the spirit of my father, which I think is within me, begins to mutiny against this servitude. I will no longer endure it, though yet I know no wise remedy how to avoid it.

10

20

Enter Oliver

ADAM Yonder comes my master, your brother.

ORLANDO Go apart, Adam, and thou shalt hear how he will shake me up.

Adam stands aside

OLIVER Now, sir, what make you here?

ORLANDO Nothing: I am not taught to make anything.

OLIVER What mar you then, sir?

30 ORLANDO Marry, sir, I am helping you to mar that which God made, a poor unworthy brother of yours, with idleness.

OLIVER Marry, sir, be better employed, and be naught a while.

ORLANDO Shall I keep your hogs and eat husks with them? What prodigal portion have I spent, that I should come to such penury?

OLIVER Know you where you are, sir?

ORLANDO O, sir, very well: here in your orchard.

40 OLIVER Know you before whom, sir?

ORLANDO Ay, better than him I am before knows me: I know you are my eldest brother, and in the gentle condition of blood you should so know me. The courtesy of nations allows you my better, in that you are the first born, but the same tradition takes not away my blood, were there twenty brothers betwixt us: I have as much of my father in me as you, albeit I confess your coming before me is nearer to his reverence.

OLIVER (*threatening him*) What, boy!

50 ORLANDO (*seizing him by the throat*) Come, come, elder brother, you are too young in this.

OLIVER Wilt thou lay hands on me, villain?

ORLANDO I am no villain: I am the youngest son of Sir Rowland de Boys; he was my father, and he is thrice a villain that says such a father begot villains. Wert thou

not my brother, I would not take this hand from thy
throat till this other had pulled out thy tongue for saying
so; thou hast railed on thyself.

ADAM (*coming forward*) Sweet masters, be patient; for
your father's remembrance, be at accord.   60

OLIVER Let me go, I say.

ORLANDO I will not till I please: you shall hear me. My
father charged you in his will to give me good education:
you have trained me like a peasant, obscuring and hiding
from me all gentleman-like qualities. The spirit of my
father grows strong in me, and I will no longer endure it.
Therefore allow me such exercises as may become a
gentleman, or give me the poor allottery my father left
me by testament; with that I will go buy my fortunes.

OLIVER And what wilt thou do, beg when that is spent?   70
Well, sir, get you in. I will not long be troubled with
you: you shall have some part of your will. I pray you,
leave me.

ORLANDO I will no further offend you than becomes me
for my good.

OLIVER Get you with him, you old dog.

ADAM Is 'old dog' my reward? Most true, I have lost my
teeth in your service. God be with my old master! He
would not have spoke such a word.

                                   Exeunt Orlando and Adam

OLIVER Is it even so? Begin you to grow upon me? I will   80
physic your rankness, and yet give no thousand crowns
neither. Holla, Dennis!

      Enter Dennis

DENNIS Calls your worship?

OLIVER Was not Charles, the Duke's wrestler, here to
speak with me?

DENNIS So please you, he is here at the door, and im-
portunes access to you.

OLIVER Call him in.   *Exit Dennis*
'Twill be a good way – and tomorrow the wrestling is.
Enter Charles

90 CHARLES Good morrow to your worship.

OLIVER Good Monsieur Charles, what's the new news at the new court?

CHARLES There's no news at the court, sir, but the old news: that is, the old Duke is banished by his younger brother the new Duke, and three or four loving lords have put themselves into voluntary exile with him, whose lands and revenues enrich the new Duke; therefore he gives them good leave to wander.

OLIVER Can you tell if Rosalind, the Duke's daughter, be
100 banished with her father?

CHARLES O, no; for the Duke's daughter, her cousin, so loves her, being ever from their cradles bred together, that she would have followed her exile, or have died to stay behind her; she is at the court, and no less beloved of her uncle than his own daughter, and never two ladies loved as they do.

OLIVER Where will the old Duke live?

CHARLES They say he is already in the Forest of Arden, and a many merry men with him; and there they live
110 like the old Robin Hood of England: they say many young gentlemen flock to him every day, and fleet the time carelessly as they did in the golden world.

OLIVER What, you wrestle tomorrow before the new Duke?

CHARLES Marry do I, sir; and I came to acquaint you with a matter. I am given, sir, secretly to understand that your younger brother, Orlando, hath a disposition to come in disguised against me to try a fall. Tomorrow, sir, I wrestle for my credit, and he that escapes me
120 without some broken limb shall acquit him well. Your

brother is but young and tender, and for your love I
would be loath to foil him, as I must for my own honour
if he come in. Therefore, out of my love to you, I came
hither to acquaint you withal, that either you might
stay him from his intendment, or brook such disgrace
well as he shall run into, in that it is a thing of his own
search, and altogether against my will.

OLIVER Charles, I thank thee for thy love to me, which
thou shalt find I will most kindly requite. I had myself
notice of my brother's purpose herein, and have by   130
underhand means laboured to dissuade him from it;
but he is resolute. I'll tell thee, Charles, it is the stubbornest young fellow of France, full of ambition, an
envious emulator of every man's good parts, a secret and
villainous contriver against me, his natural brother.
Therefore use thy discretion; I had as lief thou didst
break his neck as his finger. And thou wert best look
to't; for if thou dost him any slight disgrace, or if he
do not mightily grace himself on thee, he will practise
against thee by poison, entrap thee by some treacherous   140
device, and never leave thee till he hath ta'en thy life
by some indirect means or other: for, I assure thee –
and almost with tears I speak it – there is not one so
young and so villainous this day living. I speak but
brotherly of him, but should I anatomize him to thee
as he is, I must blush and weep, and thou must look
pale and wonder.

CHARLES I am heartily glad I came hither to you. If he
come tomorrow, I'll give him his payment: if ever he go
alone again, I'll never wrestle for prize more. And so   150
God keep your worship!   *Exit*

OLIVER Farewell, good Charles. Now will I stir this
gamester. I hope I shall see an end of him, for my soul –
yet I know not why – hates nothing more than he. Yet

he's gentle, never schooled and yet learned, full of
noble device, of all sorts enchantingly beloved, and
indeed so much in the heart of the world, and especially
of my own people, who best know him, that I am
altogether misprized. But it shall not be so long; this
160   wrestler shall clear all. Nothing remains but that I
kindle the boy thither, which now I'll go about.   *Exit*

I.2   *Enter Rosalind and Celia*

CELIA I pray thee, Rosalind, sweet my coz, be merry.

ROSALIND Dear Celia, I show more mirth than I am
mistress of, and would you yet were merrier. Unless
you could teach me to forget a banished father, you
must not learn me how to remember any extraordinary
pleasure.

CELIA Herein I see thou lovest me not with the full weight
that I love thee. If my uncle, thy banished father, had
banished thy uncle, the Duke my father, so thou hadst
10   been still with me, I could have taught my love to take
thy father for mine; so wouldst thou, if the truth of
thy love to me were so righteously tempered as mine is
to thee.

ROSALIND Well, I will forget the condition of my estate,
to rejoice in yours.

CELIA You know my father hath no child but I, nor none
is like to have; and truly, when he dies, thou shalt be his
heir: for what he hath taken away from thy father perforce, I will render thee again in affection, by mine
20   honour I will, and when I break that oath, let me turn
monster. Therefore, my sweet Rose, my dear Rose,
be merry.

ROSALIND From henceforth I will, coz, and devise sports.
Let me see – what think you of falling in love?

CELIA Marry, I prithee do, to make sport withal; but love
no man in good earnest, nor no further in sport neither,
than with safety of a pure blush thou mayst in honour
come off again.

ROSALIND What shall be our sport then?

CELIA Let us sit and mock the good housewife Fortune   30
from her wheel, that her gifts may henceforth be be-
stowed equally.

ROSALIND I would we could do so; for her benefits are
mightily misplaced, and the bountiful blind woman doth
most mistake in her gifts to women.

CELIA 'Tis true, for those that she makes fair she scarce
makes honest, and those that she makes honest she
makes very ill-favouredly.

ROSALIND Nay, now thou goest from Fortune's office to
Nature's: Fortune reigns in gifts of the world, not in   40
the lineaments of Nature.

     Enter Touchstone

CELIA No; when Nature hath made a fair creature, may
she not by Fortune fall into the fire? Though Nature
hath given us wit to flout at Fortune, hath not Fortune
sent in this fool to cut off the argument?

ROSALIND Indeed, there is Fortune too hard for Nature,
when Fortune makes Nature's natural the cutter-off of
Nature's wit.

CELIA Peradventure this is not Fortune's work neither,
but Nature's, who perceiveth our natural wits too dull   50
to reason of such goddesses and hath sent this natural
for our whetstone: for always the dullness of the fool is
the whetstone of the wits. How now, wit, whither
wander you?

TOUCHSTONE Mistress, you must come away to your
father.

CELIA Were you made the messenger?

TOUCHSTONE No, by mine honour, but I was bid to come for you.

60 ROSALIND Where learned you that oath, fool?

TOUCHSTONE Of a certain knight that swore by his honour they were good pancakes and swore by his honour the mustard was naught: now I'll stand to it the pancakes were naught and the mustard was good, and yet was not the knight forsworn.

CELIA How prove you that, in the great heap of your knowledge?

ROSALIND Ay, marry, now unmuzzle your wisdom.

TOUCHSTONE Stand you both forth now: stroke your
70 chins and swear by your beards that I am a knave.

CELIA By our beards — if we had them — thou art.

TOUCHSTONE By my knavery — if I had it — then I were; but if you swear by that that is not, you are not forsworn: no more was this knight, swearing by his honour, for he never had any; or if he had, he had sworn it away before ever he saw those pancakes or that mustard.

CELIA Prithee, who is't that thou meanest?

TOUCHSTONE One that old Frederick, your father, loves.

CELIA My father's love is enough to honour him enough.
80 Speak no more of him; you'll be whipped for taxation one of these days.

TOUCHSTONE The more pity that fools may not speak wisely what wise men do foolishly.

CELIA By my troth, thou sayest true: for since the little wit that fools have was silenced, the little foolery that wise men have makes a great show. Here comes Monsieur the Beu.

Enter Le Beau

ROSALIND With his mouth full of news.

CELIA Which he will put on us, as pigeons feed their
90 young.

ROSALIND Then shall we be news-crammed.

CELIA All the better: we shall be the more marketable.
Bon jour, Monsieur Le Beau, what's the news?

LE BEAU Fair Princess, you have lost much good sport.

CELIA Sport? Of what colour?

LE BEAU What colour, madam? How shall I answer you?

ROSALIND As wit and fortune will.

TOUCHSTONE Or as the Destinies decrees.

CELIA Well said, that was laid on with a trowel.

TOUCHSTONE Nay, if I keep not my rank —   100

ROSALIND Thou losest thy old smell.

LE BEAU You amaze me, ladies. I would have told you of
good wrestling, which you have lost the sight of.

ROSALIND Yet tell us the manner of the wrestling.

LE BEAU I will tell you the beginning; and, if it please
your ladyships, you may see the end, for the best is yet
to do, and here, where you are, they are coming to
perform it.

CELIA Well, the beginning that is dead and buried.

LE BEAU There comes an old man and his three sons —   110

CELIA I could match this beginning with an old tale.

LE BEAU Three proper young men, of excellent growth
and presence —

ROSALIND With bills on their necks: 'Be it known unto
all men by these presents.'

LE BEAU The eldest of the three wrestled with Charles,
the Duke's wrestler, which Charles in a moment threw
him, and broke three of his ribs, that there is little hope
of life in him. So he served the second, and so the third.
Yonder they lie, the poor old man their father making   120
such pitiful dole over them that all the beholders take
his part with weeping.

ROSALIND Alas!

TOUCHSTONE But what is the sport, Monsieur, that the
ladies have lost?

LE BEAU Why, this that I speak of.

TOUCHSTONE Thus men may grow wiser every day. It is
the first time that ever I heard breaking of ribs was sport
for ladies.

130 CELIA Or I, I promise thee.

ROSALIND But is there any else longs to see this broken
music in his sides? Is there yet another dotes upon rib-
breaking? Shall we see this wrestling, cousin?

LE BEAU You must if you stay here, for here is the place
appointed for the wrestling, and they are ready to perform it.

CELIA Yonder, sure, they are coming. Let us now stay
and see it.

    Flourish. Enter Duke Frederick, Lords, Orlando,
    Charles, and attendants

DUKE Come on. Since the youth will not be entreated, his
140 own peril on his forwardness.

ROSALIND Is yonder the man?

LE BEAU Even he, madam.

CELIA Alas, he is too young; yet he looks successfully.

DUKE How now, daughter and cousin? Are you crept
hither to see the wrestling?

ROSALIND Ay, my liege, so please you give us leave.

DUKE You will take little delight in it, I can tell you, there
is such odds in the man. In pity of the challenger's
youth I would fain dissuade him, but he will not be
150 entreated. Speak to him, ladies, see if you can move him.

CELIA Call him hither, good Monsieur Le Beau.

DUKE Do so: I'll not be by.

    He stands aside

LE BEAU Monsieur the challenger, the Princess calls for
you.

ORLANDO I attend them with all respect and duty.

ROSALIND Young man, have you challenged Charles the wrestler?

ORLANDO No, fair Princess. He is the general challenger; I come but in as others do, to try with him the strength of my youth.   160

CELIA Young gentleman, your spirits are too bold for your years. You have seen cruel proof of this man's strength; if you saw yourself with your eyes, or knew yourself with your judgement, the fear of your adventure would counsel you to a more equal enterprise. We pray you for your own sake to embrace your own safety, and give over this attempt.

ROSALIND Do, young sir, your reputation shall not therefore be misprized: we will make it our suit to the Duke that the wrestling might not go forward.   170

ORLANDO I beseech you, punish me not with your hard thoughts, wherein I confess me much guilty to deny so fair and excellent ladies anything. But let your fair eyes and gentle wishes go with me to my trial: wherein if I be foiled, there is but one shamed that was never gracious; if killed, but one dead that is willing to be so. I shall do my friends no wrong, for I have none to lament me; the world no injury, for in it I have nothing: only in the world I fill up a place which may be better supplied when I have made it empty.   180

ROSALIND The little strength that I have, I would it were with you.

CELIA And mine, to eke out hers.

ROSALIND Fare you well. Pray heaven, I be deceived in you!

CELIA Your heart's desires be with you!

CHARLES Come, where is this young gallant that is so desirous to lie with his mother earth?

ORLANDO Ready, sir, but his will hath in it a more
190   modest working.

DUKE You shall try but one fall.

CHARLES No, I warrant your grace, you shall not entreat
him to a second, that have so mightily persuaded him
from a first.

ORLANDO You mean to mock me after; you should not
have mocked me before. But come your ways!

ROSALIND Now Hercules be thy speed, young man!

CELIA I would I were invisible, to catch the strong fellow
by the leg.

Orlando and Charles wrestle

200   ROSALIND O excellent young man!

CELIA If I had a thunderbolt in mine eye, I can tell who
should down.

A shout as Charles is thrown

DUKE (*coming forward*) No more, no more.

ORLANDO Yes, I beseech your grace, I am not yet well
breathed.

DUKE How dost thou, Charles?

LE BEAU He cannot speak, my lord.

DUKE Bear him away.

Attendants carry Charles off

What is thy name, young man?

210   ORLANDO Orlando, my liege; the youngest son of Sir
Rowland de Boys.

DUKE

I would thou hadst been son to some man else.
The world esteemed thy father honourable,
But I did find him still mine enemy.
Thou shouldst have better pleased me with this deed
Hadst thou descended from another house.
But fare thee well, thou art a gallant youth;
I would thou hadst told me of another father.

Exit Duke, with Lords, Le Beau, and Touchstone

CELIA

　　Were I my father, coz, would I do this?

ORLANDO

　　I am more proud to be Sir Rowland's son,   220
　　His youngest son, and would not change that calling
　　To be adopted heir to Frederick.

ROSALIND

　　My father loved Sir Rowland as his soul,
　　And all the world was of my father's mind.
　　Had I before known this young man his son,
　　I should have given him tears unto entreaties
　　Ere he should thus have ventured.

CELIA   Gentle cousin,
　　Let us go thank him, and encourage him.
　　My father's rough and envious disposition
　　Sticks me at heart. — Sir, you have well deserved.   230
　　If you do keep your promises in love
　　But justly as you have exceeded all promise,
　　Your mistress shall be happy.

ROSALIND (*taking a chain from her neck*)

　　　　　　　　　　　　　　　　Gentleman,
　　Wear this for me — one out of suits with fortune,
　　That could give more but that her hand lacks means.
　　(*To Celia*) Shall we go, coz?

CELIA Ay. Fare you well, fair gentleman.

　　Rosalind and Celia begin to withdraw

ORLANDO

　　Can I not say 'I thank you'? My better parts
　　Are all thrown down, and that which here stands up
　　Is but a quintain, a mere lifeless block.   240

ROSALIND

　　He calls us back. My pride fell with my fortunes:
　　I'll ask him what he would. — Did you call, sir?

Sir, you have wrestled well, and overthrown
More than your enemies.

CELIA   Will you go, coz?

ROSALIND

Have with you. (*To Orlando*) Fare you well.

> *Exeunt Rosalind and Celia*

ORLANDO

What passion hangs these weights upon my tongue?
I cannot speak to her, yet she urged conference.

> *Enter Le Beau*

O poor Orlando, thou art overthrown!
Or Charles or something weaker masters thee.

LE BEAU

250   Good sir, I do in friendship counsel you
To leave this place. Albeit you have deserved
High commendation, true applause, and love,
Yet such is now the Duke's condition,
That he misconsters all that you have done.
The Duke is humorous — what he is, indeed,
More suits you to conceive than I to speak of.

ORLANDO

I thank you, sir; and pray you tell me this,
Which of the two was daughter of the Duke
That here was at the wrestling?

LE BEAU

260   Neither his daughter, if we judge by manners,
But yet indeed the taller is his daughter;
The other is daughter to the banished Duke,
And here detained by her usurping uncle
To keep his daughter company, whose loves
Are dearer than the natural bond of sisters.
But I can tell you that of late this Duke
Hath ta'en displeasure 'gainst his gentle niece,
Grounded upon no other argument

But that the people praise her for her virtues
And pity her for her good father's sake;   270
And, on my life, his malice 'gainst the lady
Will suddenly break forth. Sir, fare you well;
Hereafter, in a better world than this,
I shall desire more love and knowledge of you.

ORLANDO
I rest much bounden to you: fare you well.

Exit Le Beau

Thus must I from the smoke into the smother,
From tyrant Duke unto a tyrant brother.
But heavenly Rosalind!   *Exit*

Enter Celia and Rosalind   1.3

CELIA Why cousin, why Rosalind, Cupid have mercy,
not a word?

ROSALIND Not one to throw at a dog.

CELIA No, thy words are too precious to be cast away
upon curs; throw some of them at me. Come, lame me
with reasons.

ROSALIND Then there were two cousins laid up, when the
one should be lamed with reasons, and the other mad
without any.

CELIA But is all this for your father?   10

ROSALIND No, some of it is for my child's father. – O,
how full of briars is this working-day world!

CELIA They are but burs, cousin, thrown upon thee in
holiday foolery. If we walk not in the trodden paths,
our very petticoats will catch them.

ROSALIND I could shake them off my coat; these burs are
in my heart.

CELIA Hem them away.

ROSALIND I would try, if I could cry 'hem' and have
him.

CELIA Come, come, wrestle with thy affections.

ROSALIND O, they take the part of a better wrestler than
myself.

CELIA O, a good wish upon you; you will try in time, in
despite of a fall. But turning these jests out of service,
let us talk in good earnest: is it possible on such a sudden
you should fall into so strong a liking with old Sir
Rowland's youngest son?

ROSALIND The Duke my father loved his father dearly.

CELIA Doth it therefore ensue that you should love his
son dearly? By this kind of chase, I should hate him,
for my father hated his father dearly; yet I hate not
Orlando.

ROSALIND No, faith, hate him not, for my sake.

CELIA Why should I not? Doth he not deserve well?

Enter Duke, with Lords

ROSALIND Let me love him for that, and do you love him
because I do. – Look, here comes the Duke.

CELIA With his eyes full of anger.

DUKE
Mistress, dispatch you with your safest haste
And get you from our court.

ROSALIND   Me, uncle?

DUKE   You, cousin.
Within these ten days if that thou beest found
So near our public court as twenty miles,
Thou diest for it.

ROSALIND   I do beseech your grace,
Let me the knowledge of my fault bear with me.
If with myself I hold intelligence
Or have acquaintance with mine own desires,
If that I do not dream or be not frantic –

As I do trust I am not – then, dear uncle,
Never so much as in a thought unborn
Did I offend your highness.

DUKE   Thus do all traitors: 50
If their purgation did consist in words,
They are as innocent as grace itself.
Let it suffice thee that I trust thee not.

ROSALIND
Yet your mistrust cannot make me a traitor.
Tell me whereon the likelihoods depends.

DUKE
Thou art thy father's daughter, there's enough.

ROSALIND
So was I when your highness took his dukedom,
So was I when your highness banished him.
Treason is not inherited, my lord,
Or, if we did derive it from our friends,   60
What's that to me? My father was no traitor;
Then, good my liege, mistake me not so much
To think my poverty is treacherous.

CELIA
Dear sovereign, hear me speak.

DUKE
Ay, Celia, we stayed her for your sake,
Else had she with her father ranged along.

CELIA
I did not then entreat to have her stay;
It was your pleasure and your own remorse.
I was too young that time to value her,
But now I know her. If she be a traitor,   70
Why so am I: we still have slept together,
Rose at an instant, learned, played, eat together,
And wheresoe'er we went, like Juno's swans
Still we went coupled and inseparable.

DUKE
> She is too subtle for thee, and her smoothness,
> Her very silence, and her patience
> Speak to the people, and they pity her.
> Thou art a fool; she robs thee of thy name,
> And thou wilt show more bright and seem more virtuous
> When she is gone. Then open not thy lips:
> Firm and irrevocable is my doom
> Which I have passed upon her; she is banished.

CELIA
> Pronounce that sentence then on me, my liege,
> I cannot live out of her company.

DUKE
> You are a fool. — You, niece, provide yourself.
> If you outstay the time, upon mine honour
> And in the greatness of my word, you die.

> > > *Exit Duke, with Lords*

CELIA
> O my poor Rosalind, whither wilt thou go?
> Wilt thou change fathers? I will give thee mine.
> I charge thee, be not thou more grieved than I am.

ROSALIND
> I have more cause.

CELIA   Thou hast not, cousin.
> Prithee, be cheerful; knowest thou not the Duke
> Hath banished me, his daughter?

ROSALIND   That he hath not.

CELIA
> No, hath not? Rosalind lacks then the love
> Which teacheth thee that thou and I am one.
> Shall we be sundered? Shall we part, sweet girl?
> No, let my father seek another heir.
> Therefore devise with me how we may fly,

Whither to go, and what to bear with us,
And do not seek to take your change upon you,   100
To bear your griefs yourself and leave me out;
For, by this heaven, now at our sorrows pale,
Say what thou canst, I'll go along with thee.

ROSALIND

Why, whither shall we go?

CELIA

To seek my uncle in the Forest of Arden.

ROSALIND

Alas, what danger will it be to us,
Maids as we are, to travel forth so far?
Beauty provoketh thieves sooner than gold.

CELIA

I'll put myself in poor and mean attire
And with a kind of umber smirch my face.   110
The like do you; so shall we pass along
And never stir assailants.

ROSALIND   Were it not better,
Because that I am more than common tall,
That I did suit me all points like a man?
A gallant curtle-axe upon my thigh,
A boar-spear in my hand, and in my heart
Lie there what hidden woman's fear there will,
We'll have a swashing and a martial outside,
As many other mannish cowards have
That do outface it with their semblances.   120

CELIA

What shall I call thee when thou art a man?

ROSALIND

I'll have no worse a name than Jove's own page,
And therefore look you call me 'Ganymede'.
But what will you be called?

CELIA

Something that hath a reference to my state:
No longer 'Celia', but 'Aliena'.

ROSALIND

But, cousin, what if we assayed to steal
The clownish fool out of your father's court:
Would he not be a comfort to our travel?

CELIA

130   He'll go along o'er the wide world with me.
Leave me alone to woo him. Let's away
And get our jewels and our wealth together,
Devise the fittest time and safest way
To hide us from pursuit that will be made
After my flight. Now go in we content
To liberty, and not to banishment.   *Exeunt*

*

II.1   *Enter Duke Senior, Amiens, and two or three Lords*
          dressed like foresters

DUKE

Now my co-mates and brothers in exile,
Hath not old custom made this life more sweet
Than that of painted pomp? Are not these woods
More free from peril than the envious court?
Here feel we not the penalty of Adam,
The seasons' difference, as the icy fang
And churlish chiding of the winter's wind,
Which when it bites and blows upon my body
Even till I shrink with cold, I smile and say
10   'This is no flattery; these are counsellors
That feelingly persuade me what I am'?
Sweet are the uses of adversity,

Which, like the toad, ugly and venomous,
Wears yet a precious jewel in his head;
And this our life, exempt from public haunt,
Finds tongues in trees, books in the running brooks,
Sermons in stones, and good in everything.

AMIENS

I would not change it. Happy is your grace
That can translate the stubbornness of fortune
Into so quiet and so sweet a style.   20

DUKE

Come, shall we go and kill us venison?
And yet it irks me the poor dappled fools,
Being native burghers of this desert city,
Should in their own confines with forkèd heads
Have their round haunches gored.

FIRST LORD   Indeed, my lord,
The melancholy Jaques grieves at that
And, in that kind, swears you do more usurp
Than doth your brother that hath banished you.
Today my lord of Amiens and myself
Did steal behind him as he lay along   30
Under an oak whose antick root peeps out
Upon the brook that brawls along this wood,
To the which place a poor sequestered stag
That from the hunter's aim had ta'en a hurt
Did come to languish; and indeed, my lord,
The wretched animal heaved forth such groans
That their discharge did stretch his leathern coat
Almost to bursting, and the big round tears
Coursed one another down his innocent nose
In piteous chase; and thus the hairy fool,   40
Much markèd of the melancholy Jaques,
Stood on th'extremest verge of the swift brook
Augmenting it with tears.

DUKE   But what said Jaques?
Did he not moralize this spectacle?
FIRST LORD
    O, yes, into a thousand similes.
    First, for his weeping into the needless stream:
    'Poor deer,' quoth he, 'thou makest a testament
    As worldlings do, giving thy sum of more
    To that which had too much.' Then, being there alone,
50 Left and abandoned of his velvet friend,
    ''Tis right,' quoth he, 'thus misery doth part
    The flux of company.' Anon a careless herd,
    Full of the pasture, jumps along by him
    And never stays to greet him: 'Ay,' quoth Jaques,
    'Sweep on, you fat and greasy citizens,
    'Tis just the fashion! Wherefore do you look
    Upon that poor and broken bankrupt there?'
    Thus most invectively he pierceth through
    The body of country, city, court,
60 Yea, and of this our life, swearing that we
    Are mere usurpers, tyrants, and what's worse
    To fright the animals and to kill them up
    In their assigned and native dwelling place.
DUKE
    And did you leave him in this contemplation?
SECOND LORD
    We did, my lord, weeping and commenting
    Upon the sobbing deer.
DUKE   Show me the place;
    I love to cope him in these sullen fits,
    For then he's full of matter.
FIRST LORD
    I'll bring you to him straight.   *Exeunt*

Enter Duke Frederick, with Lords

DUKE

  Can it be possible that no man saw them?
  It cannot be; some villains of my court
  Are of consent and sufferance in this.

FIRST LORD

  I cannot hear of any that did see her.
  The ladies her attendants of her chamber
  Saw her abed, and in the morning early
  They found the bed untreasured of their mistress.

SECOND LORD

  My lord, the roynish clown at whom so oft
  Your grace was wont to laugh is also missing.
  Hisperia, the princess' gentlewoman,   10
  Confesses that she secretly o'erheard
  Your daughter and her cousin much commend
  The parts and graces of the wrestler
  That did but lately foil the sinewy Charles,
  And she believes wherever they are gone
  That youth is surely in their company.

DUKE

  Send to his brother; fetch that gallant hither.
  If he be absent, bring his brother to me;
  I'll make him find him. Do this suddenly,
  And let not search and inquisition quail   20
  To bring again these foolish runaways.   *Exeunt*

  Enter Orlando and Adam from opposite sides II.3

ORLANDO Who's there?

ADAM

  What, my young master? O my gentle master,
  O my sweet master, O you memory

Of old Sir Rowland, why, what make you here?
Why are you virtuous? Why do people love you?
And wherefore are you gentle, strong, and valiant?
Why would you be so fond to overcome
The bonny prizer of the humorous Duke?
Your praise is come too swiftly home before you.
Know you not, master, to some kind of men
Their graces serve them but as enemies?
No more do yours; your virtues, gentle master,
Are sanctified and holy traitors to you.
O, what a world is this, when what is comely
Envenoms him that bears it!

ORLANDO
Why, what's the matter?

ADAM   O unhappy youth,
Come not within these doors; within this roof
The enemy of all your graces lives.
Your brother – no, no brother – yet the son –
Yet not the son, I will not call him son
Of him I was about to call his father –
Hath heard your praises, and this night he means
To burn the lodging where you use to lie,
And you within it. If he fail of that,
He will have other means to cut you off.
I overheard him, and his practices.
This is no place, this house is but a butchery;
Abhor it, fear it, do not enter it.

ORLANDO
Why, whither, Adam, wouldst thou have me go?

ADAM
No matter whither, so you come not here.

ORLANDO
What, wouldst thou have me go and beg my food,
Or with a base and boisterous sword enforce

A thievish living on the common road?
This I must do, or know not what to do:
Yet this I will not do, do how I can.
I rather will subject me to the malice
Of a diverted blood and bloody brother.

ADAM

But do not so. I have five hundred crowns,
The thrifty hire I saved under your father,
Which I did store to be my foster-nurse   40
When service should in my old limbs lie lame
And unregarded age in corners thrown.
Take that, and He that doth the ravens feed,
Yea, providently caters for the sparrow,
Be comfort to my age. Here is the gold;
All this I give you. Let me be your servant.
Though I look old, yet I am strong and lusty,
For in my youth I never did apply
Hot and rebellious liquors in my blood,
Nor did not with unbashful forehead woo   50
The means of weakness and debility;
Therefore my age is as a lusty winter,
Frosty, but kindly. Let me go with you,
I'll do the service of a younger man
In all your business and necessities.

ORLANDO

O good old man, how well in thee appears
The constant service of the antique world,
When service sweat for duty, not for meed!
Thou art not for the fashion of these times,
Where none will sweat but for promotion,   60
And having that do choke their service up
Even with the having; it is not so with thee.
But, poor old man, thou prunest a rotten tree
That cannot so much as a blossom yield

In lieu of all thy pains and husbandry.
But come thy ways, we'll go along together,
And ere we have thy youthful wages spent
We'll light upon some settled low content.

ADAM

Master, go on, and I will follow thee
70   To the last gasp with truth and loyalty.
From seventeen years till now almost fourscore
Here lived I, but now live here no more.
At seventeen years many their fortunes seek,
But at fourscore it is too late a week.
Yet fortune cannot recompense me better
Than to die well, and not my master's debtor.   *Exeunt*

II.4   *Enter Rosalind as Ganymede, Celia as Aliena, and*
            the Clown, alias Touchstone

ROSALIND O Jupiter, how weary are my spirits!

TOUCHSTONE I care not for my spirits, if my legs were
    not weary.

ROSALIND I could find in my heart to disgrace my man's
    apparel, and to cry like a woman, but I must comfort the
    weaker vessel, as doublet-and-hose ought to show itself
    courageous to petticoat: therefore courage, good Aliena!

CELIA I pray you, bear with me, I cannot go no further.

TOUCHSTONE For my part, I had rather bear with you
10   than bear you: yet I should bear no cross if I did bear
    you, for I think you have no money in your purse.

ROSALIND Well, this is the Forest of Arden.

TOUCHSTONE Ay, now am I in Arden, the more fool I.
    When I was at home I was in a better place, but travel-
    lers must be content.

        Enter Corin and Silvius

ROSALIND

Ay, be so, good Touchstone. – Look you, who comes here:
A young man and an old in solemn talk.

CORIN

That is the way to make her scorn you still.

SILVIUS

O Corin, that thou knewest how I do love her!

CORIN

I partly guess, for I have loved ere now.   20

SILVIUS

No, Corin, being old thou canst not guess,
Though in thy youth thou wast as true a lover
As ever sighed upon a midnight pillow.
But if thy love were ever like to mine –
As sure I think did never man love so –
How many actions most ridiculous
Hast thou been drawn to by thy fantasy?

CORIN

Into a thousand that I have forgotten.

SILVIUS

O, thou didst then never love so heartily.
If thou rememberest not the slightest folly   30
That ever love did make thee run into,
Thou hast not loved.
Or if thou hast not sat as I do now,
Wearing thy hearer in thy mistress' praise,
Thou hast not loved.
Or if thou hast not broke from company
Abruptly, as my passion now makes me,
Thou hast not loved.
O Phebe, Phebe, Phebe!   *Exit*

ROSALIND

Alas, poor shepherd, searching of thy wound,   40
I have by hard adventure found mine own.

TOUCHSTONE And I mine. I remember when I was in love
I broke my sword upon a stone and bid him take that for
coming a-night to Jane Smile, and I remember the
kissing of her batler and the cow's dugs that her pretty
chopt hands had milked; and I remember the wooing of
a peascod instead of her, from whom I took two cods
and, giving her them again, said with weeping tears,
'Wear these for my sake.' We that are true lovers run
50   into strange capers; but as all is mortal in nature, so is
all nature in love mortal in folly.

ROSALIND Thou speakest wiser than thou art ware of.

TOUCHSTONE Nay, I shall ne'er be ware of mine own wit
till I break my shins against it.

ROSALIND
Jove, Jove! This shepherd's passion
Is much upon my fashion.

TOUCHSTONE
And mine, but it grows something stale with me.

CELIA
I pray you, one of you question yond man
If he for gold will give us any food;
60   I faint almost to death.

TOUCHSTONE Holla, you clown!

ROSALIND Peace, fool, he's not thy kinsman.

CORIN Who calls?

TOUCHSTONE Your betters, sir.

CORIN Else are they very wretched.

ROSALIND Peace, I say. Good even to you, friend.

CORIN
And to you, gentle sir, and to you all.

ROSALIND
I prithee, shepherd, if that love or gold
Can in this desert place buy entertainment,
70   Bring us where we may rest ourselves and feed.

Here's a young maid with travail much oppressed,
And faints for succour.

CORIN   Fair sir, I pity her,
And wish, for her sake more than for mine own,
My fortunes were more able to relieve her;
But I am shepherd to another man,
And do not shear the fleeces that I graze.
My master is of churlish disposition,
And little recks to find the way to heaven
By doing deeds of hospitality.
Besides, his cote, his flocks, and bounds of feed   80
Are now on sale, and at our sheepcote now,
By reason of his absence, there is nothing
That you will feed on. But what is, come see,
And in my voice most welcome shall you be.

ROSALIND
What is he that shall buy his flock and pasture?

CORIN
That young swain that you saw here but erewhile,
That little cares for buying anything.

ROSALIND
I pray thee, if it stand with honesty,
Buy thou the cottage, pasture, and the flock,
And thou shalt have to pay for it of us.   90

CELIA
And we will mend thy wages: I like this place,
And willingly could waste my time in it.

CORIN
Assuredly the thing is to be sold.
Go with me. If you like upon report
The soil, the profit, and this kind of life,
I will your very faithful feeder be,
And buy it with your gold right suddenly.   *Exeunt*

II.5   *Enter Amiens, Jaques and others*

AMIENS (*sings*)

> Under the greenwood tree,
> Who loves to lie with me,
> And turn his merry note
> Unto the sweet bird's throat:
> Come hither, come hither, come hither.
> Here shall he see
> No enemy
> But winter and rough weather.

JAQUES More, more, I prithee, more.

10 AMIENS It will make you melancholy, Monsieur Jaques.

JAQUES I thank it. More, I prithee, more. I can suck
melancholy out of a song, as a weasel sucks eggs. More,
I prithee, more.

AMIENS My voice is ragged, I know I cannot please you.

JAQUES I do not desire you to please me, I do desire you
to sing. Come, more, another stanzo. Call you 'em
'stanzos'?

AMIENS What you will, Monsieur Jaques.

JAQUES Nay, I care not for their names, they owe me
20   nothing. Will you sing?

AMIENS More at your request than to please myself.

JAQUES Well then, if ever I thank any man, I'll thank you;
but that they call 'compliment' is like th'encounter of
two dog-apes, and when a man thanks me heartily,
methinks I have given him a penny and he renders me
the beggarly thanks. Come, sing; and you that will not,
hold your tongues.

AMIENS Well, I'll end the song. – Sirs, cover the while:
the Duke will drink under this tree. – He hath been all
30   this day to look you.

JAQUES And I have been all this day to avoid him. He is
too disputable for my company: I think of as many

matters as he, but I give heaven thanks, and make no
boast of them. Come, warble, come.

ALL TOGETHER (*sing*)
   Who doth ambition shun,
   And loves to live i'th'sun,
   Seeking the food he eats,
   And pleased with what he gets:
  Come hither, come hither, come hither.
    Here shall he see   40
    No enemy
  But winter and rough weather.

JAQUES I'll give you a verse to this note, that I made
yesterday in despite of my invention.

AMIENS And I'll sing it.

JAQUES Thus it goes:
    If it do come to pass
    That any man turn ass,
    Leaving his wealth and ease,
    A stubborn will to please: 50
  Ducdame, ducdame, ducdame.
    Here shall he see
    Gross fools as he,
   An if he will come to me.

AMIENS What's that 'ducdame'?

JAQUES 'Tis a Greek invocation, to call fools into a circle.
I'll go sleep, if I can; if I cannot, I'll rail against all the
first-born of Egypt.

AMIENS And I'll go seek the Duke; his banquet is prepared.   *Exeunt* 60

Enter Orlando and Adam   II.6

ADAM Dear master, I can go no further. O, I die for food.
Here lie I down and measure out my grave. Farewell,
kind master.

ORLANDO Why, how now, Adam, no greater heart in thee?
Live a little, comfort a little, cheer thyself a little. If
this uncouth forest yield anything savage, I will either
be food for it or bring it for food to thee. Thy conceit is
nearer death than thy powers. (*Raising him*) For my sake
be comfortable; hold death a while at the arm's end. I
will here be with thee presently, and if I bring thee not
something to eat, I will give thee leave to die; but if
thou diest before I come, thou art a mocker of my
labour. Well said! Thou lookest cheerly, and I'll be with
thee quickly. Yet thou liest in the bleak air. Come, I
will bear thee to some shelter, and thou shalt not die
for lack of a dinner, if there live anything in this desert.
Cheerly, good Adam!   *Exeunt*

10

II.7   *Enter Duke Senior, Amiens, and Lords, dressed as*
            foresters, or outlaws

DUKE
    I think he be transformed into a beast,
    For I can nowhere find him like a man.
FIRST LORD
    My lord, he is but even now gone hence.
    Here was he merry, hearing of a song.
DUKE
    If he, compact of jars, grow musical,
    We shall have shortly discord in the spheres.
    Go, seek him, tell him I would speak with him.
        Enter Jaques
FIRST LORD
    He saves my labour by his own approach.
DUKE
    Why, how now, Monsieur, what a life is this,

That your poor friends must woo your company?   10
What, you look merrily?

JAQUES

A fool, a fool, I met a fool i'th'forest,
A motley fool – a miserable world! –
As I do live by food, I met a fool,
Who laid him down, and basked him in the sun,
And railed on Lady Fortune in good terms,
In good set terms, and yet a motley fool.
'Good morrow, fool,' quoth I. 'No, sir,' quoth he,
'Call me not fool till heaven hath sent me fortune.'
And then he drew a dial from his poke,   20
And looking on it, with lack-lustre eye,
Says, very wisely, 'It is ten o'clock.'
'Thus we may see', quoth he, 'how the world wags:
'Tis but an hour ago since it was nine,
And after one hour more 'twill be eleven,
And so from hour to hour we ripe, and ripe,
And then from hour to hour we rot, and rot,
And thereby hangs a tale.' When I did hear
The motley fool thus moral on the time,
My lungs began to crow like Chanticleer   30
That fools should be so deep-contemplative;
And I did laugh, sans intermission,
An hour by his dial. O noble fool!
A worthy fool: motley's the only wear!

DUKE

What fool is this?

JAQUES

A worthy fool: one that hath been a courtier,
And says, if ladies be but young and fair,
They have the gift to know it: and in his brain,
Which is as dry as the remainder biscuit

40　　After a voyage, he hath strange places crammed
With observation, the which he vents
In mangled forms. O that I were a fool!
I am ambitious for a motley coat.

DUKE
Thou shalt have one.

JAQUES　　　　　　　　It is my only suit —
Provided that you weed your better judgements
Of all opinion that grows rank in them
That I am wise. I must have liberty
Withal, as large a charter as the wind,
To blow on whom I please, for so fools have;
50　　And they that are most galled with my folly
They most must laugh. And why, sir, must they so?
The why is plain as way to parish church.
He that a fool doth very wisely hit
Doth very foolishly, although he smart,
Not to seem senseless of the bob: if not,
The wise man's folly is anatomized
Even by the squandering glances of the fool.
Invest me in my motley; give me leave
To speak my mind, and I will through and through
60　　Cleanse the foul body of th'infected world,
If they will patiently receive my medicine.

DUKE
Fie on thee! I can tell what thou wouldst do.

JAQUES
What, for a counter, would I do, but good?

DUKE
Most mischievous foul sin, in chiding sin:
For thou thyself hast been a libertine,
As sensual as the brutish sting itself,
And all th'embossèd sores and headed evils
That thou with licence of free foot hast caught

Wouldst thou disgorge into the general world.

JAQUES

    Why, who cries out on pride   70

    That can therein tax any private party?

    Doth it not flow as hugely as the sea,

    Till that the weary very means do ebb?

    What woman in the city do I name

    When that I say the city woman bears

    The cost of princes on unworthy shoulders?

    Who can come in and say that I mean her

    When such a one as she, such is her neighbour?

    Or what is he of basest function,

    That says his bravery is not on my cost,   80

    Thinking that I mean him, but therein suits

    His folly to the mettle of my speech?

    There then, how then, what then? Let me see wherein

    My tongue hath wronged him: if it do him right,

    Then he hath wronged himself; if he be free,

    Why then my taxing like a wild-goose flies,

    Unclaimed of any man. But who come here?

    Enter Orlando

ORLANDO Forbear, and eat no more.

JAQUES Why, I have eat none yet.

ORLANDO

    Nor shalt not, till necessity be served.   90

JAQUES

    Of what kind should this cock come of?

DUKE

    Art thou thus boldened, man, by thy distress

    Or else a rude despiser of good manners,

    That in civility thou seemest so empty?

ORLANDO

    You touched my vein at first: the thorny point

    Of bare distress hath ta'en from me the show

Of smooth civility; yet am I inland bred
And know some nurture. But forbear, I say,
He dies that touches any of this fruit
100   Till I and my affairs are answerèd.
JAQUES An you will not be answered with reason, I must
die.
DUKE
What would you have? Your gentleness shall force,
More than your force move us to gentleness.
ORLANDO
I almost die for food, and let me have it.
DUKE
Sit down and feed, and welcome to our table.
ORLANDO
Speak you so gently? Pardon me, I pray you.
I thought that all things had been savage here,
And therefore put I on the countenance
110   Of stern commandment. But whate'er you are
That in this desert inaccessible,
Under the shade of melancholy boughs,
Lose and neglect the creeping hours of time:
If ever you have looked on better days;
If ever been where bells have knolled to church;
If ever sat at any good man's feast;
If ever from your eyelids wiped a tear,
And know what 'tis to pity and be pitied,
Let gentleness my strong enforcement be,
120   In the which hope I blush, and hide my sword.
DUKE
True is it that we have seen better days,
And have with holy bell been knolled to church,
And sat at good men's feasts, and wiped our eyes
Of drops that sacred pity hath engendered:
And therefore sit you down in gentleness

And take upon command what help we have
That to your wanting may be ministered.

ORLANDO

Then but forbear your food a little while
Whiles, like a doe, I go to find my fawn
And give it food. There is an old poor man   130
Who after me hath many a weary step
Limped in pure love; till he be first sufficed,
Oppressed with two weak evils, age and hunger,
I will not touch a bit.

DUKE   Go find him out
And we will nothing waste till you return.

ORLANDO

I thank ye, and be blessed for your good comfort!

                                              Exit

DUKE

Thou seest we are not all alone unhappy.
This wide and universal theatre
Presents more woeful pageants than the scene
Wherein we play in.

JAQUES   All the world's a stage,   140
And all the men and women merely players;
They have their exits and their entrances,
And one man in his time plays many parts,
His Acts being seven ages. At first the infant,
Mewling and puking in the nurse's arms;
Then, the whining schoolboy, with his satchel
And shining morning face, creeping like snail
Unwillingly to school; and then the lover,
Sighing like furnace, with a woeful ballad
Made to his mistress' eyebrow; then, a soldier,   150
Full of strange oaths, and bearded like the pard,
Jealous in honour, sudden and quick in quarrel,
Seeking the bubble reputation

Even in the cannon's mouth; and then, the justice,
In fair round belly, with good capon lined,
With eyes severe, and beard of formal cut,
Full of wise saws and modern instances,
And so he plays his part; the sixth age shifts
Into the lean and slippered pantaloon,
With spectacles on nose and pouch on side,
His youthful hose, well saved, a world too wide
For his shrunk shank, and his big manly voice,
Turning again toward childish treble, pipes
And whistles in his sound; last Scene of all,
That ends this strange eventful history,
Is second childishness, and mere oblivion,
Sans teeth, sans eyes, sans taste, sans everything.

    Enter Orlando with Adam

DUKE
Welcome. Set down your venerable burden,
And let him feed.

ORLANDO
I thank you most for him.

ADAM   So had you need;
I scarce can speak to thank you for myself.

DUKE
Welcome, fall to. I will not trouble you
As yet to question you about your fortunes.
Give us some music and, good cousin, sing.

AMIENS (*sings*)
    Blow, blow, thou winter wind,
    Thou art not so unkind
        As man's ingratitude.
    Thy tooth is not so keen,
    Because thou art not seen,
        Although thy breath be rude.

160

170

180

Hey-ho, sing hey-ho, unto the green holly,
Most friendship is feigning, most loving mere folly;
    Then hey-ho, the holly,
      This life is most jolly.

    Freeze, freeze, thou bitter sky
    That dost not bite so nigh
      As benefits forgot.
    Though thou the waters warp,
    Thy sting is not so sharp
      As friend remembered not.   190
Hey-ho, sing hey-ho, unto the green holly,
Most friendship is feigning, most loving mere folly;
    Then hey-ho, the holly,
      This life is most jolly.

DUKE
If that you were the good Sir Rowland's son,
As you have whispered faithfully you were,
And as mine eye doth his effigies witness
Most truly limned and living in your face,
Be truly welcome hither. I am the Duke
That loved your father. The residue of your fortune,   200
Go to my cave and tell me. – Good old man,
Thou art right welcome as thy master is. –
Support him by the arm. Give me your hand,
And let me all your fortunes understand.   *Exeunt*

*

Enter Duke Frederick, Lords, and Oliver   III.1
DUKE
Not see him since? Sir, sir, that cannot be.
But were I not the better part made mercy,

I should not seek an absent argument
Of my revenge, thou present. But look to it,
Find out thy brother wheresoe'er he is,
Seek him with candle, bring him dead or living
Within this twelvemonth, or turn thou no more
To seek a living in our territory.
Thy lands and all things that thou dost call thine
Worth seizure do we seize into our hands
Till thou canst quit thee by thy brother's mouth
Of what we think against thee.

OLIVER

O that your highness knew my heart in this!
I never loved my brother in my life.

DUKE

More villain thou. – Well, push him out of doors,
And let my officers of such a nature
Make an extent upon his house and lands.
Do this expediently, and turn him going.   *Exeunt*

III.2   *Enter Orlando*

ORLANDO

Hang there, my verse, in witness of my love,
    And thou, thrice-crownèd queen of night, survey
With thy chaste eye, from thy pale sphere above,
    Thy huntress' name that my full life doth sway.
O Rosalind, these trees shall be my books
    And in their barks my thoughts I'll character
That every eye which in this forest looks
    Shall see thy virtue witnessed everywhere.
Run, run, Orlando, carve on every tree
The fair, the chaste, and unexpressive she.   *Exit*
    Enter Corin and Touchstone

CORIN And how like you this shepherd's life, Master
Touchstone?

TOUCHSTONE Truly, shepherd, in respect of itself, it is
a good life; but in respect that it is a shepherd's life, it
is naught. In respect that it is solitary, I like it very well;
but in respect that it is private, it is a very vile life. Now
in respect it is in the fields, it pleaseth me well; but in
respect it is not in the court, it is tedious. As it is a spare
life, look you, it fits my humour well; but as there is no
more plenty in it, it goes much against my stomach.   20
Hast any philosophy in thee, shepherd?

CORIN No more but that I know the more one sickens, the
worse at ease he is, and that he that wants money,
means, and content is without three good friends; that
the property of rain is to wet and fire to burn; that good
pasture makes fat sheep; and that a great cause of the
night is lack of the sun; that he that hath learned no wit
by nature nor art may complain of good breeding, or
comes of a very dull kindred.

TOUCHSTONE Such a one is a natural philosopher. Wast   30
ever in court, shepherd?

CORIN No, truly.

TOUCHSTONE Then thou art damned.

CORIN Nay, I hope.

TOUCHSTONE Truly thou art damned, like an ill-roasted
egg all on one side.

CORIN For not being at court? Your reason.

TOUCHSTONE Why, if thou never wast at court, thou
never sawest good manners; if thou never sawest good
manners, then thy manners must be wicked, and wicked-   40
ness is sin, and sin is damnation. Thou art in a parlous
state, shepherd.

CORIN Not a whit, Touchstone. Those that are good
manners at the court are as ridiculous in the country

as the behaviour of the country is most mockable at the court. You told me you salute not at the court but you kiss your hands; that courtesy would be uncleanly if courtiers were shepherds.

TOUCHSTONE Instance, briefly; come, instance.

50 CORIN Why, we are still handling our ewes, and their fells you know are greasy.

TOUCHSTONE Why, do not your courtier's hands sweat? And is not the grease of a mutton as wholesome as the sweat of a man? Shallow, shallow. A better instance, I say; come.

CORIN Besides, our hands are hard.

TOUCHSTONE Your lips will feel them the sooner. Shallow, again. A more sounder instance; come.

CORIN And they are often tarred over with the surgery of 60 our sheep; and would you have us kiss tar? The courtier's hands are perfumed with civet.

TOUCHSTONE Most shallow man! Thou worms' meat, in respect of a good piece of flesh indeed! Learn of the wise and perpend: civet is of a baser birth than tar, the very uncleanly flux of a cat. Mend the instance, shepherd.

CORIN You have too courtly a wit for me; I'll rest.

TOUCHSTONE Wilt thou rest damned? God help thee, shallow man! God make incision in thee, thou art raw!

CORIN Sir, I am a true labourer: I earn that I eat, get 70 that I wear, owe no man hate, envy no man's happiness, glad of other men's good, content with my harm; and the greatest of my pride is to see my ewes graze and my lambs suck.

TOUCHSTONE That is another simple sin in you, to bring the ewes and the rams together and to offer to get your living by the copulation of cattle; to be bawd to a bell-wether, and to betray a she-lamb of a twelvemonth to a crooked-pated, old, cuckoldly ram, out of all reasonable

match. If thou beest not damned for this, the devil
himself will have no shepherds. I cannot see else how   80
thou shouldst 'scape.

CORIN Here comes young Master Ganymede, my new
mistress's brother.

Enter Rosalind

ROSALIND (*reads*)
    From the east to western Ind,
    No jewel is like Rosalind.
    Her worth being mounted on the wind
    Through all the world bears Rosalind.
    All the pictures fairest lined
    Are but black to Rosalind.
    Let no face be kept in mind   90
    But the fair of Rosalind.

TOUCHSTONE I'll rhyme you so eight years together,
dinners and suppers and sleeping-hours excepted: it is
the right butter-women's rank to market.

ROSALIND Out, fool!

TOUCHSTONE For a taste:
    If a hart do lack a hind,
    Let him seek out Rosalind.
    If the cat will after kind,
    So be sure will Rosalind.   100
    Wintered garments must be lined,
    So must slender Rosalind.
    They that reap must sheaf and bind,
    Then to cart with Rosalind.
    Sweetest nut hath sourest rind,
    Such a nut is Rosalind.
    He that sweetest rose will find,
    Must find love's prick and Rosalind.
This is the very false gallop of verses. Why do you infect
yourself with them?   110

ROSALIND Peace, you dull fool, I found them on a tree.

TOUCHSTONE Truly, the tree yields bad fruit.

ROSALIND I'll graff it with you, and then I shall graff
it with a medlar; then it will be the earliest fruit
i'th'country: for you'll be rotten ere you be half ripe,
and that's the right virtue of the medlar.

TOUCHSTONE You have said; but whether wisely or no,
let the forest judge.

Enter Celia with a writing

ROSALIND Peace, here comes my sister, reading. Stand
120   aside.

CELIA (*reads*)
    Why should this a desert be?
      For it is unpeopled? No,
    Tongues I'll hang on every tree,
      That shall civil sayings show.
    Some, how brief the life of man
      Runs his erring pilgrimage,
    That the stretching of a span
      Buckles in his sum of age;
    Some, of violated vows
130   *'Twixt the souls of friend and friend;*
    But upon the fairest boughs,
      Or at every sentence end,
    Will I 'Rosalinda' write,
      Teaching all that read to know
    The quintessence of every sprite
      Heaven would in little show.
    Therefore Heaven Nature charged
      That one body should be filled
    With all graces wide-enlarged.
140   *Nature presently distilled*
    Helen's cheek, but not her heart,
      Cleopatra's majesty,

> *Atalanta's better part,*
> *   Sad Lucretia's modesty.*
> *Thus Rosalind of many parts*
> *   By heavenly synod was devised,*
> *Of many faces, eyes, and hearts,*
> *   To have the touches dearest prized.*
> *Heaven would that she these gifts should have,*
> *And I to live and die her slave.*   150

ROSALIND O most gentle Jupiter, what tedious homily of love have you wearied your parishioners withal, and never cried 'Have patience, good people!'

CELIA How now? Back, friends. – Shepherd, go off a little. – Go with him, sirrah.

TOUCHSTONE Come, shepherd, let us make an honourable retreat, though not with bag and baggage, yet with scrip and scrippage.

>   *Exit Touchstone, with Corin*

CELIA Didst thou hear these verses?

ROSALIND O, yes, I heard them all, and more too, for   160
some of them had in them more feet than the verses would bear.

CELIA That's no matter: the feet might bear the verses.

ROSALIND Ay, but the feet were lame, and could not bear themselves without the verse, and therefore stood lamely in the verse.

CELIA But didst thou hear without wondering how thy name should be hanged and carved upon these trees?

ROSALIND I was seven of the nine days out of the wonder before you came; for look here what I found on a palm-   170
tree. I was never so be-rhymed since Pythagoras' time that I was an Irish rat, which I can hardly remember.

CELIA Trow you who hath done this?

ROSALIND Is it a man?

CELIA And a chain that you once wore about his neck!
Change you colour?

ROSALIND I prithee, who?

CELIA O Lord, Lord, it is a hard matter for friends to
meet; but mountains may be removed with earthquakes
180   and so encounter.

ROSALIND Nay, but who is it?

CELIA Is it possible?

ROSALIND Nay, I prithee now with most petitionary
vehemence, tell me who it is.

CELIA O wonderful, wonderful, and most wonderful
wonderful, and yet again wonderful, and after that out of
all whooping!

ROSALIND Good my complexion! Dost thou think,
though I am caparisoned like a man, I have a doublet
190   and hose in my disposition? One inch of delay more is a
South Sea of discovery. I prithee tell me who is it
quickly, and speak apace. I would thou couldst stammer,
that thou mightst pour this concealed man out of thy
mouth as wine comes out of a narrow-mouthed bottle:
either too much at once, or none at all. I prithee take
the cork out of thy mouth, that I may drink thy tidings.

CELIA So you may put a man in your belly.

ROSALIND Is he of God's making? What manner of
man? Is his head worth a hat? Or his chin worth a
200   beard?

CELIA Nay, he hath but a little beard.

ROSALIND Why, God will send more, if the man will be
thankful. Let me stay the growth of his beard, if thou
delay me not the knowledge of his chin.

CELIA It is young Orlando, that tripped up the wrestler's
heels and your heart, both in an instant.

ROSALIND Nay, but the devil take mocking; speak sad
brow and true maid.

CELIA I'faith, coz, 'tis he.

ROSALIND Orlando?   210

CELIA Orlando.

ROSALIND Alas the day, what shall I do with my doublet
and hose? What did he when thou sawest him? What
said he? How looked he? Wherein went he? What
makes he here? Did he ask for me? Where remains he?
How parted he with thee? And when shalt thou see
him again? Answer me in one word.

CELIA You must borrow me Gargantua's mouth first: 'tis
a word too great for any mouth of this age's size. To
say 'ay' and 'no' to these particulars is more than to   220
answer in a catechism.

ROSALIND But doth he know that I am in this forest and
in man's apparel? Looks he as freshly as he did the
day he wrestled?

CELIA It is as easy to count atomies as to resolve the
propositions of a lover; but take a taste of my finding
him, and relish it with good observance. I found him
under a tree like a dropped acorn.

ROSALIND It may well be called Jove's tree, when it
drops such fruit.   230

CELIA Give me audience, good madam.

ROSALIND Proceed.

CELIA There lay he, stretched along like a wounded
knight.

ROSALIND Though it be pity to see such a sight, it well
becomes the ground.

CELIA Cry 'holla' to thy tongue, I prithee; it curvets
unseasonably. He was furnished like a hunter.

ROSALIND O ominous! He comes to kill my heart.

CELIA I would sing my song without a burden. Thou   240
bringest me out of tune.

ROSALIND Do you not know I am a woman? When I
think, I must speak. Sweet, say on.
 Enter Orlando and Jaques
CELIA You bring me out. Soft, comes he not here?
ROSALIND 'Tis he. Slink by, and note him.
 Celia and Rosalind stand back
JAQUES I thank you for your company, but, good faith,
I had as lief have been myself alone.
ORLANDO And so had I; but yet, for fashion sake, I thank
you too for your society.

250 JAQUES God buy you, let's meet as little as we can.

ORLANDO I do desire we may be better strangers.

JAQUES I pray you, mar no more trees with writing love-
songs in their barks.

ORLANDO I pray you, mar no moe of my verses with
reading them ill-favouredly.

JAQUES Rosalind is your love's name?

ORLANDO Yes, just.

JAQUES I do not like her name.

ORLANDO There was no thought of pleasing you when
260 she was christened.

JAQUES What stature is she of?

ORLANDO Just as high as my heart.

JAQUES You are full of pretty answers: have you not been
acquainted with goldsmiths' wives, and conned them
out of rings?

ORLANDO Not so; but I answer you right painted cloth,
from whence you have studied your questions.

JAQUES You have a nimble wit; I think 'twas made of
Atalanta's heels. Will you sit down with me, and we two
270 will rail against our mistress the world, and all our
misery?

ORLANDO I will chide no breather in the world but myself, against whom I know most faults.

JAQUES The worst fault you have is to be in love.

ORLANDO 'Tis a fault I will not change for your best virtue. I am weary of you.

JAQUES By my troth, I was seeking for a fool when I found you.

ORLANDO He is drowned in the brook; look but in and you shall see him.   280

JAQUES There I shall see mine own figure.

ORLANDO Which I take to be either a fool or a cipher.

JAQUES I'll tarry no longer with you. Farewell, good Signor Love.

ORLANDO I am glad of your departure. Adieu, good Monsieur Melancholy.

Exit Jaques

ROSALIND (*to Celia*) I will speak to him like a saucy lackey, and under that habit play the knave with him. – Do you hear, forester?

ORLANDO Very well. What would you?   290

ROSALIND I pray you, what is't o'clock?

ORLANDO You should ask me what time o'day: there's no clock in the forest.

ROSALIND Then there is no true lover in the forest, else sighing every minute and groaning every hour would detect the lazy foot of Time as well as a clock.

ORLANDO And why not the swift foot of Time? Had not that been as proper?

ROSALIND By no means, sir: Time travels in divers paces with divers persons. I'll tell you who Time   300 ambles withal, who Time trots withal, who Time gallops withal, and who he stands still withal.

ORLANDO I prithee, who doth he trot withal?

ROSALIND Marry, he trots hard with a young maid between the contract of her marriage and the day it is solemnized. If the interim be but a se'nnight, Time's pace is so hard that it seems the length of seven year.

ORLANDO Who ambles Time withal?

ROSALIND With a priest that lacks Latin, and a rich man
that hath not the gout: for the one sleeps easily because
he cannot study, and the other lives merrily because he
feels no pain, the one lacking the burden of lean and
wasteful learning, the other knowing no burden of
heavy tedious penury. These Time ambles withal.

ORLANDO Who doth he gallop withal?

ROSALIND With a thief to the gallows: for though he go
as softly as foot can fall, he thinks himself too soon
there.

ORLANDO Who stays it still withal?

ROSALIND With lawyers in the vacation: for they sleep
between term and term, and then they perceive not how
Time moves.

ORLANDO Where dwell you, pretty youth?

ROSALIND With this shepherdess, my sister, here in the
skirts of the forest, like fringe upon a petticoat.

ORLANDO Are you native of this place?

ROSALIND As the cony that you see dwell where she is
kindled.

ORLANDO Your accent is something finer than you could
purchase in so removed a dwelling.

ROSALIND I have been told so of many; but indeed an old
religious uncle of mine taught me to speak, who was in
his youth an inland man – one that knew courtship too
well, for there he fell in love. I have heard him read
many lectures against it, and I thank God I am not a
woman, to be touched with so many giddy offences as
he hath generally taxed their whole sex withal.

ORLANDO Can you remember any of the principal evils
that he laid to the charge of women?

ROSALIND There were none principal, they were all like

one another as halfpence are, every one fault seeming
monstrous till his fellow-fault came to match it.

ORLANDO I prithee, recount some of them.

ROSALIND No, I will not cast away my physic but on
those that are sick. There is a man haunts the forest
that abuses our young plants with carving 'Rosalind' on
their barks; hangs odes upon hawthorns, and elegies on
brambles; all, forsooth, deifying the name of Rosalind.
If I could meet that fancy-monger, I would give him
some good counsel, for he seems to have the quotidian   350
of love upon him.

ORLANDO I am he that is so love-shaked. I pray you, tell
me your remedy.

ROSALIND There is none of my uncle's marks upon you.
He taught me how to know a man in love; in which cage
of rushes I am sure you are not prisoner.

ORLANDO What were his marks?

ROSALIND A lean cheek, which you have not; a blue eye
and sunken, which you have not; an unquestionable
spirit, which you have not; a beard neglected, which   360
you have not – but I pardon you for that, for simply
your having in beard is a younger brother's revenue.
Then your hose should be ungartered, your bonnet
unbanded, your sleeve unbuttoned, your shoe untied,
and everything about you demonstrating a careless
desolation. But you are no such man: you are rather
point-device in your accoutrements, as loving yourself,
than seeming the lover of any other.

ORLANDO Fair youth, I would I could make thee believe
I love.   370

ROSALIND Me believe it? You may as soon make her that
you love believe it, which I warrant she is apter to do
than to confess she does: that is one of the points in the
which women still give the lie to their consciences. But

in good sooth, are you he that hangs the verses on the
trees, wherein Rosalind is so admired?

ORLANDO I swear to thee, youth, by the white hand of
Rosalind, I am that he, that unfortunate he.

ROSALIND But are you so much in love as your rhymes
380   speak?

ORLANDO Neither rhyme nor reason can express how
much.

ROSALIND Love is merely a madness and, I tell you,
deserves as well a dark house and a whip as madmen do;
and the reason why they are not so punished and cured
is that the lunacy is so ordinary that the whippers are
in love too. Yet I profess curing it by counsel.

ORLANDO Did you ever cure any so?

ROSALIND Yes, one, and in this manner. He was to
390   imagine me his love, his mistress; and I set him every
day to woo me. At which time would I, being but a
moonish youth, grieve, be effeminate, changeable,
longing and liking, proud, fantastical, apish, shallow,
inconstant, full of tears, full of smiles; for every passion
something, and for no passion truly anything, as boys
and women are for the most part cattle of this colour;
would now like him, now loathe him; then entertain
him, then forswear him; now weep for him, then spit
at him; that I drave my suitor from his mad humour of
400   love to a living humour of madness — which was, to
forswear the full stream of the world and to live in a
nook merely monastic. And thus I cured him, and this
way will I take upon me to wash your liver as clean as a
sound sheep's heart, that there shall not be one spot of
love in't.

ORLANDO I would not be cured, youth.

ROSALIND I would cure you, if you would but call me

'Rosalind', and come every day to my cote, and woo me.

ORLANDO Now, by the faith of my love, I will. Tell me
    where it is.   410

ROSALIND Go with me to it and I'll show it you: and by
    the way you shall tell me where in the forest you live.
    Will you go?

ORLANDO With all my heart, good youth.

ROSALIND Nay, you must call me 'Rosalind'. – Come,
    sister, will you go?   *Exeunt*

Enter Touchstone and Audrey, followed by Jaques   III.3

TOUCHSTONE Come apace, good Audrey. I will fetch up
    your goats, Audrey. And now, Audrey, am I the man
    yet? Doth my simple feature content you?

AUDREY Your features, Lord warrant us! What features?

TOUCHSTONE I am here with thee and thy goats, as the
    most capricious poet, honest Ovid, was among the
    Goths.

JAQUES (*aside*) O knowledge ill-inhabited, worse than Jove
    in a thatched house!

TOUCHSTONE When a man's verses cannot be understood,   10
    nor a man's good wit seconded with the forward child
    Understanding, it strikes a man more dead than a great
    reckoning in a little room. Truly, I would the gods had
    made thee poetical.

AUDREY I do not know what 'poetical' is. Is it honest in
    deed and word? Is it a true thing?

TOUCHSTONE No, truly: for the truest poetry is the most
    feigning; and lovers are given to poetry; and what they
    swear in poetry may be said as lovers they do feign.

AUDREY Do you wish then that the gods had made me   20
    poetical?

TOUCHSTONE I do, truly: for thou swearest to me thou art
honest; now, if thou wert a poet, I might have some hope
thou didst feign.

AUDREY Would you not have me honest?

TOUCHSTONE No, truly, unless thou wert hard-favoured:
for honesty coupled to beauty is to have honey a sauce
to sugar.

JAQUES (*aside*) A material fool!

30 AUDREY Well, I am not fair, and therefore I pray the gods
make me honest.

TOUCHSTONE Truly, and to cast away honesty upon a
foul slut were to put good meat into an unclean dish.

AUDREY I am not a slut, though I thank the gods I am
foul.

TOUCHSTONE Well, praised be the gods for thy foulness;
sluttishness may come hereafter. But be it as it may be, I
will marry thee; and to that end, I have been with Sir
Oliver Martext, the vicar of the next village, who hath
40 promised to meet me in this place of the forest and to
couple us.

JAQUES (*aside*) I would fain see this meeting.

AUDREY Well, the gods give us joy.

TOUCHSTONE Amen. A man may, if he were of a fearful
heart, stagger in this attempt; for here we have no temple
but the wood, no assembly but horn-beasts. But what
though? Courage! As horns are odious, they are necessary. It is said, 'Many a man knows no end of his goods.'
Right! Many a man has good horns, and knows no end
50 of them. Well, that is the dowry of his wife, 'tis none of
his own getting. Horns? Even so. Poor men alone? No,
no, the noblest deer hath them as huge as the rascal.
Is the single man therefore blessed? No. As a walled
town is more worthier than a village, so is the forehead
of a married man more honourable than the bare brow

of a bachelor; and by how much defence is better than no skill, by so much is a horn more precious than to want.

Enter Sir Oliver Martext

Here comes Sir Oliver. – Sir Oliver Martext, you are well met. Will you dispatch us here under this tree, or 60 shall we go with you to your chapel?

SIR OLIVER Is there none here to give the woman?

TOUCHSTONE I will not take her on gift of any man.

SIR OLIVER Truly, she must be given, or the marriage is not lawful.

JAQUES (*coming forward*) Proceed, proceed; I'll give her.

TOUCHSTONE Good even, good Master What-ye-call't: how do you, sir? You are very well met. God 'ild you for your last company, I am very glad to see you. Even a toy in hand here, sir. Nay, pray be covered. 70

JAQUES Will you be married, motley?

TOUCHSTONE As the ox hath his bow, sir, the horse his curb, and the falcon her bells, so man hath his desires; and as pigeons bill, so wedlock would be nibbling.

JAQUES And will you, being a man of your breeding, be married under a bush like a beggar? Get you to church, and have a good priest that can tell you what marriage is. This fellow will but join you together as they join wainscot; then one of you will prove a shrunk panel and, like green timber, warp, warp. 80

TOUCHSTONE I am not in the mind but I were better to be married of him than of another, for he is not like to marry me well; and not being well married, it will be a good excuse for me hereafter to leave my wife.

JAQUES Go thou with me, and let me counsel thee.

TOUCHSTONE Come, sweet Audrey, we must be married, or we must live in bawdry. Farewell, good Master Oliver. Not

> *O sweet Oliver,*
> *O brave Oliver,*
> *Leave me not behind thee*

but

> *Wind away,*
> *Be gone, I say,*
> *I will not to wedding with thee.*

SIR OLIVER (*aside*) 'Tis no matter; ne'er a fantastical knave of them all shall flout me out of my calling.

Exeunt

III.4   *Enter Rosalind and Celia*

ROSALIND Never talk to me, I will weep.

CELIA Do, I prithee, but yet have the grace to consider that tears do not become a man.

ROSALIND But have I not cause to weep?

CELIA As good cause as one would desire; therefore weep.

ROSALIND His very hair is of the dissembling colour.

CELIA Something browner than Judas's. Marry, his kisses are Judas's own children.

ROSALIND I'faith, his hair is of a good colour.

CELIA An excellent colour: your chestnut was ever the only colour.

ROSALIND And his kissing is as full of sanctity as the touch of holy bread.

CELIA He hath bought a pair of cast lips of Diana. A nun of winter's sisterhood kisses not more religiously; the very ice of chastity is in them.

ROSALIND But why did he swear he would come this morning, and comes not?

CELIA Nay, certainly, there is no truth in him.

ROSALIND Do you think so?

CELIA Yes, I think he is not a pick-purse nor a horse-

stealer, but for his verity in love I do think him as
concave as a covered goblet or a worm-eaten nut.

ROSALIND Not true in love?

CELIA Yes, when he is in — but I think he is not in.

ROSALIND You have heard him swear downright he was.

CELIA 'Was' is not 'is'. Besides, the oath of lover is no
stronger than the word of a tapster: they are both the
confirmer of false reckonings. He attends here in the
forest on the Duke your father.   30

ROSALIND I met the Duke yesterday and had much
question with him. He asked me of what parentage I
was. I told him, of as good as he — so he laughed and let
me go. But what talk we of fathers, when there is such a
man as Orlando?

CELIA O, that's a brave man! He writes brave verses,
speaks brave words, swears brave oaths and breaks
them bravely, quite traverse, athwart the heart of his
lover, as a puisny tilter that spurs his horse but on one
side breaks his staff like a noble goose. But all's brave   40
that youth mounts and folly guides. Who comes here?

    Enter Corin

CORIN
    Mistress and master, you have oft inquired
    After the shepherd that complained of love,
    Who you saw sitting by me on the turf,
    Praising the proud disdainful shepherdess
    That was his mistress.

CELIA   Well: and what of him?

CORIN
    If you will see a pageant truly played,
    Between the pale complexion of true love
    And the red glow of scorn and proud disdain,
    Go hence a little and I shall conduct you,   50
    If you will mark it.

ROSALIND   O come, let us remove;
 The sight of lovers feedeth those in love.
 Bring us to this sight, and you shall say
 I'll prove a busy actor in their play. *Exeunt*

III.5 *Enter Silvius and Phebe*

SILVIUS
 Sweet Phebe, do not scorn me, do not, Phebe.
 Say that you love me not, but say not so
 In bitterness. The common executioner,
 Whose heart th'accustomed sight of death makes hard,
 Falls not the axe upon the humbled neck
 But first begs pardon: will you sterner be
 Than he that dies and lives by bloody drops?
  Enter Rosalind, Celia, and Corin, unobserved

PHEBE
 I would not be thy executioner.
 I fly thee, for I would not injure thee.
10 Thou tellest me there is murder in mine eye:
 'Tis pretty, sure, and very probable,
 That eyes, that are the frail'st and softest things,
 Who shut their coward gates on atomies,
 Should be called tyrants, butchers, murderers!
 Now I do frown on thee with all my heart,
 And if mine eyes can wound, now let them kill thee.
 Now counterfeit to swoon, why now fall down,
 Or if thou canst not, O for shame, for shame,
 Lie not, to say mine eyes are murderers!
20 Now show the wound mine eye hath made in thee.
 Scratch thee but with a pin, and there remains
 Some scar of it; lean upon a rush,
 The cicatrice and capable impressure
 Thy palm some moment keeps; but now mine eyes,

Which I have darted at thee, hurt thee not,
Nor, I am sure, there is no force in eyes
That can do hurt.

SILVIUS   O dear Phebe,
If ever — as that ever may be near —
You meet in some fresh cheek the power of fancy,
Then shall you know the wounds invisible   30
That love's keen arrows make.

PHEBE   But till that time
Come not thou near me; and when that time comes,
Afflict me with thy mocks, pity me not,
As till that time I shall not pity thee.

ROSALIND (*coming forward*)
And why, I pray you? Who might be your mother,
That you insult, exult and all at once
Over the wretched? What, though you have no beauty —
As, by my faith, I see no more in you
Than without candle may go dark to bed —
Must you be therefore proud and pitiless?   40
Why, what means this? Why do you look on me?
I see no more in you than in the ordinary
Of nature's sale-work. 'Od's my little life,
I think she means to tangle my eyes too!
No, faith, proud mistress, hope not after it:
'Tis not your inky brows, your black silk hair,
Your bugle eyeballs, nor your cheek of cream
That can entame my spirits to your worship.
You foolish shepherd, wherefore do you follow her,
Like foggy south, puffing with wind and rain?   50
You are a thousand times a properer man
Than she a woman. 'Tis such fools as you
That makes the world full of ill-favoured children.
'Tis not her glass but you that flatters her,
And out of you she sees herself more proper

Than any of her lineaments can show her.
But, mistress, know yourself; down on your knees
And thank heaven, fasting, for a good man's love!
For I must tell you friendly in your ear,
Sell when you can, you are not for all markets.
Cry the man mercy, love him, take his offer.
Foul is most foul, being foul to be a scoffer.
So take her to thee, shepherd. Fare you well.

PHEBE

Sweet youth, I pray you chide a year together;
I had rather hear you chide than this man woo.

ROSALIND (*to Phebe*) He's fallen in love with your foulness,
(*to Silvius*) and she'll fall in love with my anger. If it
be so, as fast as she answers thee with frowning looks,
I'll sauce her with bitter words. (*To Phebe*) Why look
you so upon me?

PHEBE

For no ill will I bear you.

ROSALIND

I pray you, do not fall in love with me,
For I am falser than vows made in wine.
Besides, I like you not. (*To Silvius*) If you will know
      my house,
'Tis at the tuft of olives here hard by. —
Will you go, sister? — Shepherd, ply her hard. —
Come, sister. — Shepherdess, look on him better,
And be not proud, though all the world could see,
None could be so abused in sight as he.
Come, to our flock.

                    Exit Rosalind, with Celia and Corin

PHEBE

Dead Shepherd, now I find thy saw of might,
'Who ever loved that loved not at first sight?'

SILVIUS
　Sweet Phebe –
PHEBE　　　　　　Ha, what sayest thou, Silvius?
SILVIUS
　Sweet Phebe, pity me.
PHEBE
　Why, I am sorry for thee, gentle Silvius.
SILVIUS
　Wherever sorrow is, relief would be.
　If you do sorrow at my grief in love,
　By giving love, your sorrow and my grief
　Were both extermined.
PHEBE
　Thou hast my love; is not that neighbourly?　　　90
SILVIUS
　I would have you.
PHEBE　　　　　　Why, that were covetousness.
　Silvius, the time was that I hated thee,
　And yet it is not that I bear thee love;
　But since that thou canst talk of love so well,
　Thy company, which erst was irksome to me,
　I will endure, and I'll employ thee too.
　But do not look for further recompense
　Than thine own gladness that thou art employed.
SILVIUS
　So holy and so perfect is my love,
　And I in such a poverty of grace,　　　　　　　100
　That I shall think it a most plenteous crop
　To glean the broken ears after the man
　That the main harvest reaps. Loose now and then
　A scattered smile, and that I'll live upon.
PHEBE
　Knowest thou the youth that spoke to me erewhile?

SILVIUS
    Not very well, but I have met him oft,
    And he hath bought the cottage and the bounds
    That the old carlot once was master of.

PHEBE
    Think not I love him, though I ask for him.
110   'Tis but a peevish boy. Yet he talks well.
    But what care I for words? Yet words do well
    When he that speaks them pleases those that hear.
    It is a pretty youth – not very pretty –
    But, sure, he's proud – and yet his pride becomes him.
    He'll make a proper man. The best thing in him
    Is his complexion; and faster than his tongue
    Did make offence, his eye did heal it up.
    He is not very tall – yet for his years he's tall.
    His leg is but so so – and yet 'tis well.
120   There was a pretty redness in his lip,
    A little riper and more lusty red
    Than that mixed in his cheek; 'twas just the difference
    Betwixt the constant red and mingled damask.
    There be some women, Silvius, had they marked him
    In parcels, as I did, would have gone near
    To fall in love with him: but, for my part,
    I love him not, nor hate him not; and yet
    I have more cause to hate him than to love him,
    For what had he to do to chide at me?
130   He said mine eyes were black and my hair black,
    And, now I am remembered, scorned at me;
    I marvel why I answered not again.
    But that's all one: omittance is no quittance;
    I'll write to him a very taunting letter,
    And thou shalt bear it – wilt thou, Silvius?

SILVIUS
    Phebe, with all my heart.

PHEBE   I'll write it straight:
The matter's in my head and in my heart.
I will be bitter with him and passing short.
Go with me, Silvius.   *Exeunt*

*

Enter Rosalind, Celia, and Jaques   IV. 1

JAQUES I prithee, pretty youth, let me be better acquainted
    with thee.

ROSALIND They say you are a melancholy fellow.

JAQUES I am so: I do love it better than laughing.

ROSALIND Those that are in extremity of either are
    abominable fellows, and betray themselves to every
    modern censure worse than drunkards.

JAQUES Why, 'tis good to be sad and say nothing.

ROSALIND Why then, 'tis good to be a post.

JAQUES I have neither the scholar's melancholy, which is   10
    emulation; nor the musician's, which is fantastical; nor
    the courtier's, which is proud; nor the soldier's, which is
    ambitious; nor the lawyer's, which is politic; nor the
    lady's, which is nice; nor the lover's, which is all these:
    but it is a melancholy of mine own, compounded of
    many simples, extracted from many objects, and indeed
    the sundry contemplation of my travels, in which my
    often rumination wraps me in a most humorous sadness.

ROSALIND A traveller! By my faith, you have great
    reason to be sad. I fear you have sold your own lands to   20
    see other men's; then, to have seen much and to have
    nothing is to have rich eyes and poor hands.

JAQUES Yes, I have gained my experience.
    Enter Orlando

ROSALIND And your experience makes you sad. I had

rather have a fool to make me merry than experience to make me sad – and to travail for it too!

ORLANDO
Good day, and happiness, dear Rosalind!

JAQUES Nay then, God buy you, an you talk in blank verse. (*Going*)

ROSALIND (*as he goes*) Farewell, Monsieur Traveller. Look
30   you lisp and wear strange suits; disable all the benefits of your own country; be out of love with your nativity, and almost chide God for making you that countenance you are; or I will scarce think you have swam in a gondola. – Why, how now, Orlando, where have you been all this while? You a lover! An you serve me such another trick, never come in my sight more.

ORLANDO My fair Rosalind, I come within an hour of my promise.

ROSALIND Break an hour's promise in love? He that will
40   divide a minute into a thousand parts, and break but a part of the thousandth part of a minute in the affairs of love, it may be said of him that Cupid hath clapped him o'th'shoulder, but I'll warrant him heart-whole.

ORLANDO Pardon me, dear Rosalind.

ROSALIND Nay, an you be so tardy come no more in my sight; I had as lief be wooed of a snail.

ORLANDO Of a snail?

ROSALIND Ay, of a snail: for though he comes slowly, he carries his house on his head – a better jointure, I think,
50   than you make a woman. Besides, he brings his destiny with him.

ORLANDO What's that?

ROSALIND Why, horns; which such as you are fain to be beholding to your wives for. But he comes armed in his fortune, and prevents the slander of his wife.

ORLANDO Virtue is no horn-maker; and my Rosalind is
virtuous.

ROSALIND And I am your Rosalind.

CELIA It pleases him to call you so; but he hath a Rosalind
of a better leer than you.   60

ROSALIND Come, woo me, woo me: for now I am in a
holiday humour, and like enough to consent. What
would you say to me now, an I were your very, very
Rosalind?

ORLANDO I would kiss before I spoke.

ROSALIND Nay, you were better speak first, and when you
were gravelled for lack of matter, you might take occasion
to kiss. Very good orators, when they are out, they will
spit, and for lovers lacking – God warn us! – matter, the
cleanliest shift is to kiss.   70

ORLANDO How if the kiss be denied?

ROSALIND Then she puts you to entreaty, and there
begins new matter.

ORLANDO Who could be out, being before his beloved
mistress?

ROSALIND Marry, that should you if I were your mistress,
or I should think my honesty ranker than my wit.

ORLANDO What, of my suit?

ROSALIND Not out of your apparel, and yet out of your
suit. Am not I your Rosalind?   80

ORLANDO I take some joy to say you are, because I would
be talking of her.

ROSALIND Well, in her person, I say I will not have you.

ORLANDO Then, in mine own person, I die.

ROSALIND No, faith, die by attorney. The poor world is
almost six thousand years old, and in all this time there
was not any man died in his own person, videlicet, in a
love-cause. Troilus had his brains dashed out with a
Grecian club, yet he did what he could to die before,

90   and he is one of the patterns of love. Leander, he would
      have lived many a fair year though Hero had turned
      nun, if it had not been for a hot midsummer night: for,
      good youth, he went but forth to wash him in the
      Hellespont and being taken with the cramp was drowned,
      and the foolish chroniclers of that age found it was 'Hero
      of Sestos'. But these are all lies; men have died from
      time to time and worms have eaten them, but not for
      love.

ORLANDO I would not have my right Rosalind of this
100   mind, for I protest her frown might kill me.

ROSALIND By this hand, it will not kill a fly. But come,
      now I will be your Rosalind in a more coming-on
      disposition; and ask me what you will, I will grant it.

ORLANDO Then love me, Rosalind.

ROSALIND Yes, faith will I, Fridays and Saturdays and
      all.

ORLANDO And wilt thou have me?

ROSALIND Ay, and twenty such.

ORLANDO What sayest thou?

110   ROSALIND Are you not good?

ORLANDO I hope so.

ROSALIND Why then, can one desire too much of a good
      thing? Come, sister, you shall be the priest and marry
      us. – Give me your hand, Orlando. – What do you say,
      sister?

ORLANDO Pray thee, marry us.

CELIA I cannot say the words.

ROSALIND You must begin 'Will you, Orlando'.

CELIA Go to. – Will you, Orlando, have to wife this
120   Rosalind?

ORLANDO I will.

ROSALIND Ay, but when?

ORLANDO Why, now, as fast as she can marry us.

ROSALIND Then you must say 'I take thee, Rosalind, for wife.'

ORLANDO I take thee, Rosalind, for wife.

ROSALIND I might ask you for your commission, but I do take thee, Orlando, for my husband. There's a girl goes before the priest, and certainly a woman's thought runs before her actions.   130

ORLANDO So do all thoughts, they are winged.

ROSALIND Now tell me how long you would have her after you have possessed her.

ORLANDO For ever and a day.

ROSALIND Say 'a day' without the 'ever'. No, no, Orlando, men are April when they woo, December when they wed; maids are May when they are maids, but the sky changes when they are wives. I will be more jealous of thee than a Barbary cock-pigeon over his hen, more clamorous than a parrot against rain, more new-fangled   140 than an ape, more giddy in my desires than a monkey; I will weep for nothing, like Diana in the fountain, and I will do that when you are disposed to be merry; I will laugh like a hyen, and that when thou art inclined to sleep.

ORLANDO But will my Rosalind do so?

ROSALIND By my life, she will do as I do.

ORLANDO O, but she is wise.

ROSALIND Or else she could not have the wit to do this. The wiser, the waywarder. Make the doors upon a   150 woman's wit, and it will out at the casement; shut that, and 'twill out at the key-hole; stop that, 'twill fly with the smoke out at the chimney.

ORLANDO A man that had a wife with such a wit, he might say 'Wit, whither wilt?'

ROSALIND Nay, you might keep that check for it, till you met your wife's wit going to your neighbour's bed.

ORLANDO And what wit could wit have to excuse that?

ROSALIND Marry, to say she came to seek you there. You
160   shall never take her without her answer, unless you take
her without her tongue. O, that woman that cannot make
her fault her husband's occasion, let her never nurse her
child herself, for she will breed it like a fool.

ORLANDO For these two hours, Rosalind, I will leave thee.

ROSALIND Alas, dear love, I cannot lack thee two hours!

ORLANDO I must attend the Duke at dinner. By two
o'clock I will be with thee again.

ROSALIND Ay, go your ways, go your ways: I knew what
you would prove, my friends told me as much, and I
170   thought no less. That flattering tongue of yours won
me. 'Tis but one cast away, and so, come death. Two
o'clock is your hour?

ORLANDO Ay, sweet Rosalind.

ROSALIND By my troth, and in good earnest, and so God
mend me, and by all pretty oaths that are not dangerous,
if you break one jot of your promise, or come one minute
behind your hour, I will think you the most pathetical
break-promise, and the most hollow lover, and the most
unworthy of her you call Rosalind, that may be chosen
180   out of the gross band of the unfaithful. Therefore,
beware my censure, and keep your promise.

ORLANDO With no less religion than if thou wert indeed
my Rosalind. So, adieu.

ROSALIND Well, Time is the old justice that examines all
such offenders, and let Time try. Adieu! *Exit Orlando*

CELIA You have simply misused our sex in your love-
prate. We must have your doublet and hose plucked
over your head, and show the world what the bird hath
done to her own nest.

190   ROSALIND O coz, coz, coz, my pretty little coz, that thou
didst know how many fathom deep I am in love! But it

cannot be sounded: my affection hath an unknown bottom, like the Bay of Portugal.

CELIA Or rather, bottomless, that as fast as you pour affection in, it runs out.

ROSALIND No, that same wicked bastard of Venus, that was begot of thought, conceived of spleen, and born of madness, that blind rascally boy that abuses everyone's eyes because his own are out, let him be judge how deep I am in love. I'll tell thee, Aliena, I cannot be out   200 of the sight of Orlando: I'll go find a shadow and sigh till he come.

CELIA And I'll sleep.   *Exeunt*

Enter Jaques, and Lords dressed as foresters   IV.2

JAQUES Which is he that killed the deer?

LORD Sir, it was I.

JAQUES Let's present him to the Duke like a Roman conqueror. And it would do well to set the deer's horns upon his head for a branch of victory. Have you no song, forester, for this purpose?

LORD Yes, sir.

JAQUES Sing it. 'Tis no matter how it be in tune, so it make noise enough.

    Music

LORDS   *Song*

        What shall he have that killed the deer?
        His leather skin and horns to wear.   10
        Then sing him home, the rest shall bear
        This burden.
        Take thou no scorn to wear the horn,
        It was a crest ere thou wast born,
              Thy father's father wore it,
              And thy father bore it,

The horn, the horn, the lusty horn,
Is not a thing to laugh to scorn.   *Exeunt*

IV.3   *Enter Rosalind and Celia*

ROSALIND How say you now? Is it not past two o'clock?
      And here much Orlando!

CELIA I warrant you, with pure love and troubled brain
      he hath ta'en his bow and arrows, and is gone forth to
      sleep.
          Enter Silvius
      Look who comes here.

SILVIUS
      My errand is to you, fair youth:
      My gentle Phebe did bid me give you this.
          He gives Rosalind a letter, which she reads
      I know not the contents, but as I guess
10   By the stern brow and waspish action
      Which she did use as she was writing of it,
      It bears an angry tenor. Pardon me,
      I am but as a guiltless messenger.

ROSALIND
      Patience herself would startle at this letter,
      And play the swaggerer. Bear this, bear all.
      She says I am not fair, that I lack manners,
      She calls me proud, and that she could not love me
      Were man as rare as phoenix. 'Od's my will,
      Her love is not the hare that I do hunt!
20   Why writes she so to me? Well, shepherd, well,
      This is a letter of your own device.

SILVIUS
      No, I protest, I know not the contents;
      Phebe did write it.

ROSALIND   Come, come, you are a fool,

And turned into the extremity of love.
I saw her hand: she has a leathern hand,
A freestone-coloured hand; I verily did think
That her old gloves were on, but 'twas her hands;
She has a housewife's hand – but that's no matter.
I say she never did invent this letter;
This is a man's invention, and his hand.   30

SILVIUS
Sure, it is hers.

ROSALIND
Why, 'tis a boisterous and a cruel style,
A style for challengers. Why, she defies me,
Like Turk to Christian; women's gentle brain
Could not drop forth such giant rude invention,
Such Ethiop words, blacker in their effect
Than in their countenance. Will you hear the letter?

SILVIUS
So please you, for I never heard it yet;
Yet heard too much of Phebe's cruelty.

ROSALIND
She Phebes me; mark how the tyrant writes·   40
    Art thou god to shepherd turned,
    That a maiden's heart hath burned?
Can a woman rail thus?

SILVIUS Call you this railing?

ROSALIND
    Why, thy godhead laid apart,
    Warrest thou with a woman's heart?
Did you ever hear such railing?
    Whiles the eye of man did woo me,
    That could do no vengeance to me.
Meaning me a beast.   50
    If the scorn of your bright eyne
    Have power to raise such love in mine,

Alack, in me what strange effect
Would they work in mild aspect?
Whiles you chid me, I did love,
How then might your prayers move?
He that brings this love to thee
Little knows this love in me;
And by him seal up thy mind,
60   *Whether that thy youth and kind*
Will the faithful offer take
Of me and all that I can make,
Or else by him my love deny,
And then I'll study how to die.

SILVIUS Call you this chiding?

CELIA Alas, poor shepherd!

ROSALIND Do you pity him? No, he deserves no pity. –
Wilt thou love such a woman? What, to make thee an
instrument and play false strains upon thee? Not to be
70   endured! Well, go your way to her – for I see love hath
made thee a tame snake – and say this to her: that if
she love me, I charge her to love thee; if she will not,
I will never have her, unless thou entreat for her. If
you be a true lover, hence, and not a word, for here
comes more company.

Exit Silvius

Enter Oliver

OLIVER
Good morrow, fair ones. Pray you, if you know,
Where in the purlieus of this forest stands
A sheepcote fenced about with olive trees?

CELIA
West of this place, down in the neighbour bottom,
80   The rank of osiers by the murmuring stream
Left on your right hand brings you to the place.
But at this hour the house doth keep itself,

There's none within.

OLIVER

If that an eye may profit by a tongue,
Then should I know you by description.
Such garments and such years: 'The boy is fair,
Of female favour, and bestows himself
Like a ripe sister; the woman low
And browner than her brother.' Are not you
The owner of the house I did inquire for?   90

CELIA

It is no boast, being asked, to say we are.

OLIVER

Orlando doth commend him to you both,
And to that youth he calls his 'Rosalind'
He sends this bloody napkin. Are you he?

ROSALIND

I am. What must we understand by this?

OLIVER

Some of my shame, if you will know of me
What man I am, and how, and why, and where
This handkercher was stained.

CELIA   I pray you, tell it.

OLIVER

When last the young Orlando parted from you,
He left a promise to return again   100
Within an hour; and pacing through the forest,
Chewing the food of sweet and bitter fancy,
Lo, what befell! He threw his eye aside,
And mark what object did present itself!
Under an oak, whose boughs were mossed with age
And high top bald with dry antiquity,
A wretched ragged man, o'ergrown with hair,
Lay sleeping on his back. About his neck
A green and gilded snake had wreathed itself,

110 Who with her head nimble in threats approached
The opening of his mouth; but suddenly,
Seeing Orlando, it unlinked itself
And with indented glides did slip away
Into a bush: under which bush's shade
A lioness, with udders all drawn dry,
Lay couching, head on ground, with catlike watch
When that the sleeping man should stir; for 'tis
The royal disposition of that beast
To prey on nothing that doth seem as dead.
120 This seen, Orlando did approach the man,
And found it was his brother, his elder brother.

CELIA

O, I have heard him speak of that same brother,
And he did render him the most unnatural
That lived amongst men.

OLIVER   And well he might so do,
For well I know he was unnatural.

ROSALIND

But to Orlando: did he leave him there,
Food to the sucked and hungry lioness?

OLIVER

Twice did he turn his back and purposed so.
But kindness, nobler ever than revenge,
130 And nature, stronger than his just occasion,
Made him give battle to the lioness,
Who quickly fell before him; in which hurtling
From miserable slumber I awaked.

CELIA

Are you his brother?

ROSALIND   Was't you he rescued?

CELIA

Was't you that did so oft contrive to kill him?

OLIVER

'Twas I, but 'tis not I: I do not shame
To tell you what I was, since my conversion
So sweetly tastes, being the thing I am.

ROSALIND

But, for the bloody napkin?

OLIVER   By and by.

When from the first to last betwixt us two   140
Tears our recountments had most kindly bathed,
As how I came into that desert place –
I'brief, he led me to the gentle Duke,
Who gave me fresh array and entertainment,
Committing me unto my brother's love,
Who led me instantly unto his cave,
There stripped himself, and here upon his arm
The lioness had torn some flesh away,
Which all this while had bled; and now he fainted,
And cried, in fainting, upon Rosalind.   150
Brief, I recovered him, bound up his wound,
And after some small space, being strong at heart,
He sent me hither, stranger as I am,
To tell this story, that you might excuse
His broken promise, and to give this napkin,
Dyed in this blood, unto the shepherd youth
That he in sport doth call his 'Rosalind'.

    Rosalind faints

CELIA

Why, how now, Ganymede, sweet Ganymede!

OLIVER

Many will swoon when they do look on blood.

CELIA

There is more in it. – Cousin Ganymede!   160

OLIVER

Look, he recovers.

ROSALIND
> I would I were at home.

CELIA   We'll lead you thither. –
> I pray you, will you take him by the arm?

OLIVER Be of good cheer, youth! You a man? You lack
a man's heart.

ROSALIND I do so, I confess it. Ah, sirrah, a body would
think this was well counterfeited. I pray you, tell your
brother how well I counterfeited. Heigh-ho!

OLIVER This was not counterfeit, there is too great testi-
170   mony in your complexion that it was a passion of earnest.

ROSALIND Counterfeit, I assure you.

OLIVER Well then, take a good heart, and counterfeit to
be a man.

ROSALIND So I do; but, i'faith, I should have been a
woman by right.

CELIA Come, you look paler and paler. Pray you, draw
homewards. – Good sir, go with us.

OLIVER
> That will I: for I must bear answer back
> How you excuse my brother, Rosalind.

180   ROSALIND I shall devise something. But I pray you
commend my counterfeiting to him. Will you go?

> *Exeunt*

*

V. I   *Enter Touchstone and Audrey*

TOUCHSTONE We shall find a time, Audrey. Patience,
gentle Audrey.

AUDREY Faith, the priest was good enough, for all the old
gentleman's saying.

TOUCHSTONE A most wicked Sir Oliver, Audrey, a most

vile Martext. But, Audrey, there is a youth here in the
forest lays claim to you.

AUDREY Ay, I know who 'tis: he hath no interest in me in
the world. Here comes the man you mean.

Enter William

TOUCHSTONE It is meat and drink to me to see a clown.   10
By my troth, we that have good wits have much to answer
for: we shall be flouting, we cannot hold.

WILLIAM Good even, Audrey.

AUDREY God ye good even, William.

WILLIAM And good even to you, sir.

TOUCHSTONE Good even, gentle friend. Cover thy head,
cover thy head; nay, prithee, be covered. How old are
you, friend?

WILLIAM Five-and-twenty, sir.

TOUCHSTONE A ripe age. Is thy name William?   20

WILLIAM William, sir.

TOUCHSTONE A fair name. Wast born i'th'forest here?

WILLIAM Ay, sir, I thank God.

TOUCHSTONE 'Thank God': a good answer. Art rich?

WILLIAM Faith, sir, so so.

TOUCHSTONE 'So so' is good, very good, very excellent
good; and yet it is not, it is but so so. Art thou wise?

WILLIAM Ay, sir, I have a pretty wit.

TOUCHSTONE Why, thou sayest well. I do now remember
a saying: 'The fool doth think he is wise, but the wise   30
man knows himself to be a fool.' The heathen philosopher, when he had a desire to eat a grape, would open
his lips when he put it into his mouth, meaning thereby
that grapes were made to eat and lips to open. You do
love this maid?

WILLIAM I do, sir.

TOUCHSTONE Give me your hand. Art thou learned?

WILLIAM No, sir.

TOUCHSTONE Then learn this of me. To have is to have.
40   For it is a figure in rhetoric that drink, being poured out
      of a cup into a glass, by filling the one doth empty the
      other; for all your writers do consent that 'ipse' is he.
      Now, you are not 'ipse', for I am he.
WILLIAM Which he, sir?
TOUCHSTONE He, sir, that must marry this woman.
      Therefore, you clown, abandon – which is in the vulgar
      'leave' – the society – which in the boorish is 'company' –
      of this female – which in the common is 'woman' –
      which, together, is 'abandon the society of this female',
50   or, clown, thou perishest; or, to thy better understand-
      ing, diest; or, to wit, I kill thee, make thee away,
      translate thy life into death, thy liberty into bondage.
      I will deal in poison with thee, or in bastinado, or in
      steel; I will bandy with thee in faction; I will o'er-run
      thee with policy; I will kill thee a hundred and fifty
      ways – therefore tremble and depart.
AUDREY Do, good William.
WILLIAM God rest you merry, sir.   *Exit*
      Enter Corin
CORIN Our master and mistress seeks you: come away,
60   away.
TOUCHSTONE Trip, Audrey, trip, Audrey. I attend, I
      attend.   *Exeunt*

V.2   *Enter Orlando and Oliver*
ORLANDO Is't possible, that on so little acquaintance you
      should like her? That, but seeing, you should love her?
      And loving woo? And, wooing, she should grant? And
      will you persever to enjoy her?
OLIVER Neither call the giddiness of it in question: the
      poverty of her, the small acquaintance, my sudden

wooing, nor her sudden consenting; but say with me
'I love Aliena'; say with her that she loves me; consent
with both that we may enjoy each other. It shall be to
your good, for my father's house and all the revenue   10
that was old Sir Rowland's will I estate upon you, and
here live and die a shepherd.

    Enter Rosalind

ORLANDO You have my consent. Let your wedding be
tomorrow. Thither will I invite the Duke and all's
contented followers. Go you and prepare Aliena; for,
look you, here comes my Rosalind.

ROSALIND God save you, brother.

OLIVER And you, fair sister.   *Exit*

ROSALIND O my dear Orlando, how it grieves me to see
thee wear thy heart in a scarf.   20

ORLANDO It is my arm.

ROSALIND I thought thy heart had been wounded with
the claws of a lion.

ORLANDO Wounded it is, but with the eyes of a lady.

ROSALIND Did your brother tell you how I counterfeited
to sound, when he showed me your handkercher?

ORLANDO Ay, and greater wonders than that.

ROSALIND O, I know where you are. Nay, 'tis true; there
was never anything so sudden but the fight of two rams,
and Caesar's thrasonical brag of 'I came, saw, and over-   30
came'. For your brother and my sister no sooner met
but they looked; no sooner looked but they loved; no
sooner loved but they sighed; no sooner sighed but they
asked one another the reason; no sooner knew the
reason but they sought the remedy: and in these
degrees have they made a pair of stairs to marriage
which they will climb incontinent or else be incontinent
before marriage. They are in the very wrath of love and
they will together; clubs cannot part them.

40 ORLANDO They shall be married tomorrow; and I will
    bid the Duke to the nuptial. But, O, how bitter a thing
    it is to look into happiness through another man's eyes!
    By so much the more shall I tomorrow be at the height
    of heart-heaviness, by how much I shall think my
    brother happy in having what he wishes for.

    ROSALIND Why, then, tomorrow I cannot serve your
    turn for Rosalind?

    ORLANDO I can live no longer by thinking.

    ROSALIND I will weary you then no longer with idle
50 talking. Know of me then, for now I speak to some
    purpose, that I know you are a gentleman of good con-
    ceit. I speak not this that you should bear a good
    opinion of my knowledge, insomuch I say I know you
    are; neither do I labour for a greater esteem than may
    in some little measure draw a belief from you to do
    yourself good, and not to grace me. Believe then, if you
    please, that I can do strange things: I have, since I was
    three year old, conversed with a magician, most pro-
    found in his art, and yet not damnable. If you do love
60 Rosalind so near the heart as your gesture cries it out,
    when your brother marries Aliena, shall you marry her.
    I know into what straits of fortune she is driven, and it
    is not impossible to me, if it appear not inconvenient
    to you, to set her before your eyes tomorrow, human as
    she is, and without any danger.

    ORLANDO Speakest thou in sober meanings?

    ROSALIND By my life I do, which I tender dearly though
    I say I am a magician. Therefore, put you in your best
    array, bid your friends; for if you will be married to-
70 morrow, you shall; and to Rosalind, if you will.
        Enter Silvius and Phebe
    Look, here comes a lover of mine and a lover of hers.

PHEBE
    Youth, you have done me much ungentleness,
    To show the letter that I writ to you.

ROSALIND
    I care not if I have: it is my study
    To seem despiteful and ungentle to you.
    You are there followed by a faithful shepherd;
    Look upon him, love him: he worships you.

PHEBE
    Good shepherd, tell this youth what 'tis to love.

SILVIUS
    It is to be all made of sighs and tears,
    And so am I for Phebe.   80

PHEBE
    And I for Ganymede.

ORLANDO
    And I for Rosalind.

ROSALIND
    And I for no woman.

SILVIUS
    It is to be all made of faith and service,
    And so am I for Phebe.

PHEBE
    And I for Ganymede.

ORLANDO
    And I for Rosalind.

ROSALIND
    And I for no woman.

SILVIUS
    It is to be all made of fantasy,
    All made of passion, and all made of wishes,   90
    All adoration, duty and observance,
    All humbleness, all patience, and impatience,
    All purity, all trial, all observance;

And so am I for Phebe.

PHEBE
And so am I for Ganymede.

ORLANDO
And so am I for Rosalind.

ROSALIND
And so am I for no woman.

PHEBE (*to Rosalind*)
If this be so, why blame you me to love you?

SILVIUS (*to Phebe*)
If this be so, why blame you me to love you?

ORLANDO
If this be so, why blame you me to love you?

ROSALIND Why do you speak too 'Why blame you me to
love you?'

ORLANDO
To her that is not here, nor doth not hear.

ROSALIND Pray you no more of this, 'tis like the howling
of Irish wolves against the moon. (*To Silvius*) I will
help you, if I can. (*To Phebe*) I would love you, if I
could. – Tomorrow meet me all together. (*To Phebe*) I
will marry you if ever I marry woman, and I'll be
married tomorrow. (*To Orlando*) I will satisfy you, if
ever I satisfied man, and you shall be married tomorrow.
(*To Silvius*) I will content you, if what pleases you
contents you, and you shall be married tomorrow. (*To
Orlando*) As you love Rosalind, meet. (*To Silvius*) As
you love Phebe, meet. – And as I love no woman, I'll
meet. So, fare you well; I have left you commands.

SILVIUS I'll not fail, if I live.

PHEBE Nor I.

ORLANDO Nor I.   *Exeunt*

Enter Touchstone and Audrey

TOUCHSTONE Tomorrow is the joyful day, Audrey. Tomorrow will we be married.

AUDREY I do desire it with all my heart; and I hope it is no dishonest desire to desire to be a woman of the world? Here come two of the banished Duke's pages.

Enter two Pages

FIRST PAGE Well met, honest gentleman.

TOUCHSTONE By my troth, well met. Come, sit, sit, and a song.

SECOND PAGE We are for you. Sit i'th'middle.

FIRST PAGE Shall we clap into't roundly, without hawk-   10
ing, or spitting, or saying we are hoarse, which are the only prologues to a bad voice?

SECOND PAGE I'faith, i'faith; and both in a tune, like two gypsies on a horse.

PAGES   *Song*

It was a lover and his lass,
    With a hey, and a ho, and a hey nonino,
That o'er the green corn field did pass,
    In the spring time, the only pretty ring time,
When birds do sing, hey ding a ding, ding,
Sweet lovers love the spring.   20

Between the acres of the rye,
    With a hey, and a ho, and a hey nonino,
These pretty country folks would lie,
    In spring time, the only pretty ring time,
    When birds do sing, hey ding a ding, ding,
    Sweet lovers love the spring.

This carol they began that hour,
    With a hey, and a ho, and a hey nonino,
How that a life was but a flower,
        In spring time, the only pretty ring time,
When birds do sing, hey ding a ding, ding,
Sweet lovers love the spring.

And therefore take the present time,
    With a hey, and a ho, and a hey nonino,
For love is crownèd with the prime,
        In spring time, the only pretty ring time,
When birds do sing, hey ding a ding, ding,
Sweet lovers love the spring.

TOUCHSTONE Truly, young gentlemen, though there was
no great matter in the ditty, yet the note was very
untuneable.

FIRST PAGE You are deceived, sir; we kept time, we lost
not our time.

TOUCHSTONE By my troth, yes: I count it but time lost to
hear such a foolish song. God buy you, and God mend
your voices! Come, Audrey.   *Exeunt*

V.4   *Enter Duke Senior, Amiens, Jaques, Orlando, Oliver,*
           and Celia

DUKE
Dost thou believe, Orlando, that the boy
Can do all this that he hath promised?

ORLANDO
I sometimes do believe, and sometimes do not,
As those that fear they hope, and know they fear.
    Enter Rosalind, Silvius, and Phebe

ROSALIND
Patience once more, whiles our compact is urged.

(To the Duke) You say, if I bring in your Rosalind,
You will bestow her on Orlando here?

DUKE

That would I, had I kingdoms to give with her.

ROSALIND *(to Orlando)*

And you say you will have her, when I bring her?

ORLANDO

That would I, were I of all kingdoms king.   10

ROSALIND *(to Phebe)*

You say you'll marry me, if I be willing?

PHEBE

That will I, should I die the hour after.

ROSALIND

But if you do refuse to marry me,
You'll give yourself to this most faithful shepherd?

PHEBE

So is the bargain.

ROSALIND *(to Silvius)*

You say that you'll have Phebe, if she will?

SILVIUS

Though to have her and death were both one thing.

ROSALIND

I have promised to make all this matter even.
Keep you your word, O Duke, to give your daughter;
You yours, Orlando, to receive his daughter;   20
Keep you your word, Phebe, that you'll marry me
Or else, refusing me, to wed this shepherd;
Keep your word, Silvius, that you'll marry her,
If she refuse me – and from hence I go,
To make these doubts all even.

Exeunt Rosalind and Celia

DUKE

I do remember in this shepherd boy
Some lively touches of my daughter's favour.

ORLANDO
>My lord, the first time that I ever saw him
>Methought he was a brother to your daughter.
30 >But, my good lord, this boy is forest-born,
>And hath been tutored in the rudiments
>Of many desperate studies by his uncle,
>Whom he reports to be a great magician,
>>*Enter Touchstone and Audrey*
>Obscurèd in the circle of this forest.

JAQUES There is sure another flood toward, and these couples are coming to the ark. Here comes a pair of very strange beasts, which in all tongues are called fools.

TOUCHSTONE Salutation and greeting to you all!

JAQUES Good my lord, bid him welcome: this is the
40 motley-minded gentleman that I have so often met in the forest. He hath been a courtier, he swears.

TOUCHSTONE If any man doubt that, let him put me to my purgation. I have trod a measure, I have flattered a lady, I have been politic with my friend, smooth with mine enemy, I have undone three tailors, I have had four quarrels, and like to have fought one.

JAQUES And how was that ta'en up?

TOUCHSTONE Faith, we met, and found the quarrel was upon the seventh cause.

50 JAQUES How seventh cause? – Good my lord, like this fellow.

DUKE I like him very well.

TOUCHSTONE God 'ild you, sir, I desire you of the like. I press in here, sir, amongst the rest of the country copulatives, to swear and to forswear, according as marriage binds and blood breaks. A poor virgin, sir, an ill-favoured thing, sir, but mine own, a poor humour of mine, sir, to take that that no man else will. Rich honesty

dwells like a miser, sir, in a poor house, as your pearl in
your foul oyster.   60

DUKE By my faith, he is very swift and sententious.

TOUCHSTONE According to the fool's bolt, sir, and such
dulcet diseases.

JAQUES But for the seventh cause. How did you find the
quarrel on the seventh cause?

TOUCHSTONE Upon a lie seven times removed. – Bear
your body more seeming, Audrey. – As thus, sir. I did
dislike the cut of a certain courtier's beard. He sent me
word, if I said his beard was not cut well, he was in the
mind it was: this is called the Retort Courteous. If I   70
sent him word again it was not well cut, he would send
me word he cut it to please himself: this is called the
Quip Modest. If again 'it was not well cut', he disabled
my judgement: this is called the Reply Churlish. If
again 'it was not well cut', he would answer, I spake not
true: this is called the Reproof Valiant. If again 'it was
not well cut', he would say, I lie: this is called the
Countercheck Quarrelsome: and so to Lie Circumstantial and the Lie Direct.

JAQUES And how oft did you say his beard was not well   80
cut?

TOUCHSTONE I durst go no further than the Lie Circumstantial, nor he durst not give me the Lie Direct. And
so we measured swords and parted.

JAQUES Can you nominate in order now the degrees of the
lie?

TOUCHSTONE O sir, we quarrel in print, by the book, as
you have books for good manners. I will name you the
degrees. The first, the Retort Courteous; the second,
the Quip Modest; the third, the Reply Churlish; the   90
fourth, the Reproof Valiant; the fifth, the Counter-

check Quarrelsome; the sixth, the Lie with Circumstance; the seventh, the Lie Direct. All these you may
avoid but the Lie Direct; and you may avoid that too,
with an 'If'. I knew when seven justices could not take
up a quarrel, but when the parties were met themselves,
one of them thought but of an 'If': as, 'If you said so,
then I said so'; and they shook hands and swore
brothers. Your 'If' is the only peace-maker; much
virtue in 'If'.

JAQUES Is not this a rare fellow, my lord? He's as good
at anything, and yet a fool.

DUKE He uses his folly like a stalking-horse, and under the
presentation of that he shoots his wit.

> *Enter a masquer representing Hymen, and Rosalind
> and Celia as themselves. Still music*

HYMEN
        Then is there mirth in heaven,
        When earthly things, made even,
                Atone together.
        Good Duke, receive thy daughter,
        Hymen from heaven brought her,
                Yea, brought her hither
        That thou mightst join her hand with his
        Whose heart within her bosom is.

ROSALIND (*to the Duke*)
        To you I give myself, for I am yours.
        (*To Orlando*)
        To you I give myself, for I am yours.

DUKE
        If there be truth in sight, you are my daughter.

ORLANDO
        If there be truth in sight, you are my Rosalind.

PHEBE
        If sight and shape be true,
        Why then, my love adieu!

ROSALIND *(to the Duke)*
  I'll have no father, if you be not he;
  (to Orlando)
  I'll have no husband, if you be not he;   120
  (to Phebe)
  Nor ne'er wed woman, if you be not she.
HYMEN
  Peace, ho! I bar confusion.
  'Tis I must make conclusion
      Of these most strange events.
  Here's eight that must take hands,
  To join in Hymen's bands,
      If truth holds true contents.
  (To Orlando and Rosalind)
  You and you no cross shall part;
  (to Oliver and Celia)
  You and you are heart in heart;
  (to Phebe)
  You to his love must accord,   130
  Or have a woman to your lord;
  (to Touchstone and Audrey)
  You and you are sure together,
  As the winter to foul weather.
  Whiles a wedlock-hymn we sing,
  Feed yourselves with questioning,
  That reason wonder may diminish
  How thus we met, and these things finish
                      Song
          Wedding is great Juno's crown,
              O blessèd bond of board and bed;
          'Tis Hymen peoples every town,   140
              High wedlock then be honourèd;
          Honour, high honour and renown
          To Hymen, god of every town!

DUKE

    O my dear niece, welcome thou art to me,

    Even daughter, welcome, in no less degree.

PHEBE (*to Silvius*)

    I will not eat my word, now thou art mine,

    Thy faith my fancy to thee doth combine.

    Enter Second Brother, Jaques de Boys

JAQUES DE BOYS

    Let me have audience for a word or two.

    I am the second son of old Sir Rowland

150   That bring these tidings to this fair assembly.

    Duke Frederick, hearing how that every day

    Men of great worth resorted to this forest,

    Addressed a mighty power, which were on foot,

    In his own conduct, purposely to take

    His brother here and put him to the sword;

    And to the skirts of this wild wood he came,

    Where, meeting with an old religious man,

    After some question with him, was converted

    Both from his enterprise and from the world,

160   His crown bequeathing to his banished brother,

    And all their lands restored to them again

    That were with him exiled. This to be true,

    I do engage my life.

DUKE   Welcome, young man.

    Thou offerest fairly to thy brothers' wedding:

    To one his lands withheld, and to the other

    A land itself at large, a potent dukedom.

    First, in this forest, let us do those ends

    That here were well begun and well begot;

    And after, every of this happy number

170   That have endured shrewd days and nights with us

    Shall share the good of our returnèd fortune

    According to the measure of their states.

Meantime, forget this new-fallen dignity,
And fall into our rustic revelry:
Play, music, and you brides and bridegrooms all,
With measure heaped in joy, to th'measures fall.

JAQUES

Sir, by your patience. – If I heard you rightly,
The Duke hath put on a religious life,
And thrown into neglect the pompous court?

JAQUES DE BOYS

He hath.   180

JAQUES

To him will I: out of these convertites
There is much matter to be heard and learned.
(*To the Duke*)
You to your former honour I bequeath:
Your patience and your virtue well deserves it;
(*to Orlando*)
You to a love that your true faith doth merit;
(*to Oliver*)
You to your land, and love, and great allies;
(*to Silvius*)
You to a long and well deservèd bed;
(*to Touchstone*)
And you to wrangling, for thy loving voyage
Is but for two months victualled. – So to your pleasures:
I am for other than for dancing measures.   190

DUKE

Stay, Jaques, stay.

JAQUES

To see no pastime, I. What you would have
I'll stay to know at your abandoned cave.   *Exit*

DUKE

Proceed, proceed. We'll begin these rites
As we do trust they'll end, in true delights.

Exeunt all except Rosalind

ROSALIND It is not the fashion to see the lady the epilogue, but it is no more unhandsome than to see the lord the prologue. If it be true that good wine needs no bush, 'tis true that a good play needs no epilogue. Yet to good wine they do use good bushes, and good plays prove the better by the help of good epilogues. What a case am I in, then, that am neither a good epilogue nor cannot insinuate with you in the behalf of a good play? I am not furnished like a beggar; therefore to beg will not become me. My way is to conjure you, and I'll begin with the women. I charge you, O women, for the love you bear to men, to like as much of this play as please you; and I charge you, O men, for the love you bear to women – as I perceive by your simpering, none of you hates them – that between you and the women the play may please. If I were a woman, I would kiss as many of you as had beards that pleased me, complexions that liked me, and breaths that I defied not; and, I am sure, as many as have good beards, or good faces, or sweet breaths, will, for my kind offer, when I make curtsy, bid me farewell.   *Exit*

An Account of the Text

As You Like It was first published in the great collection of Shakespeare's plays made after his death, the first Folio of 1623 (hereafter called F). The entry of the play on the Stationers' Register on 4 August 1600 'to be staied' may indicate an intention to prevent publication by others rather than an intention by Shakespeare's company to print it themselves; certainly no publication followed, and the play was duly entered on the Register again on 8 November 1623, among the F plays 'not formerly entred to other men'.

The F text was probably based on an authorial manuscript (or a transcript of one) that had been used in the theatre and then prepared for publication (hence the division into acts and scenes). As Charlton Hinman has demonstrated in *The Printing and Proof-Reading of the First Folio of Shakespeare* (1963), the text was set up by no fewer than three different compositors ('B', 'C' and 'D'), probably setting copy simultaneously for much of the time. (The evidence is from differing spelling habits as well as typography.) Accordingly the copy had to be 'cast off' (that is, calculation had to be made in advance of how much printed space a certain amount of the manuscript would take); and if the calculation was wrong, prose could be spun out to look like verse (as seems to have happened in II.6 and III.4) or verse could be printed as prose.

There was some sporadic proof-correcting, on three of the twenty-three pages, as the sheets were being run off; and, in the usual Elizabethan fashion, the incorrect sheets were retained and used as well as those corrected. Hence different copies of F have different readings on three pages (193, 204 and 207), but none of the nine alterations would have required reference to copy. The only two variants of even minor interest are the speech ascriptions of V.1.20 and 21, originally given in error to *Orl.* and *Clo.* (Touchstone) and corrected to *Clo.* and *Will.* respectively.

The emendations made in the second, third, and fourth Folios (all in the seventeenth century) are sometimes correct but have no more authority than the emendations of later editors (beginning with Rowe in 1709). Accordingly they are not listed separately here.

COLLATIONS

1

The following emendations of F have been accepted in this edition (the F reading is given after the square bracket, in the original spelling, except that the 'long s' (∫) has been replaced by 's'). Obvious printer's errors and mislineation (such as that in II.6 and III.4) are not listed; stage directions are treated separately in Collation 3.

I.1

    103 she] hee
    152 OLIVER] *not in* F

I.2

    51 and hath] hath
    79 CELIA] *Ros.*
    278 Rosalind!] *Rosaline.*

II.1

    49 much] must

II.3

    10 some] seeme
    16 ORLANDO] *not in* F
    29 ORLANDO] *Ad.*
    71 seventeen] seauentie

II.4

    1 weary] merry
  16–17 Ay . . . here: | A . . . talk] *prose in* F

 40 thy wound] they would
 66 you, friend] your friend
91–2 And ... place, | And ... it] And ... wages: | I ...
     could | Waste ... it

II.5

  1 AMIENS (*sings*)] Song (*above the first line*)
6–7 Here ... see | No enemy] *one line in* F
11–13 (*prose*)] I ... prethee more, | I ... song, | As ...
     more
15–17 (*prose*)] I ... me, | I ... sing: | Come ... stanzo's
31–4 (*prose*)] And ... him: | He ... companie: | I ... giue |
     Heauen ... them. | Come ... come
43–4 (*prose*)] Ile ... note, | That ... Inuention
 46 JAQUES] *Amy.*
52–3 Here ... see | Gross ... he] *one line in* F
59–60 (*prose*)] And ... Duke, | His ... prepar'd

II.7

 36 A worthy] O worthie
 55 Not to seem] Seeme
101–2 (*prose*)] An ... reason, | I ... dye
103–4 What ... force, | More ... gentleness] What ... haue? |
     Your ... your force | Moue ...gentlenesse
168–9 Welcome ... burdon, | And ... feed] *prose in* F
 175 AMIENS (*sings*)] Song
 183 Then hey-ho] *The heigh ho*

III.2

 121 *a desert*] *Desert*
     be?] *bee,*
 141 her] *his*
 230 such] forth F1; forth such F2
 237 thy] the
246–7 (*prose*)] I ... faith | I ... alone
248–9 (*prose*)] And ... sake | I ... societie
 348 deifying] defying

III.3

  2 now] how
 51 Horns? Even so. Poor men alone?] hornes, euen so
     poore men alone:
 85 (*prose*)] Go ... mee, | And ... thee

86–95 Come ... *with thee*] Come ... *Audrey*, | We ...
baudrey: | Farewel ... Not O ... *Oliuer*, O ... *Oliuer*
leaue ... thee: But winde away, bee ... say, I ... with
thee

III.5

128 I have] Haue

IV.1

1 me be] me
17–18 my often] by often
195 in, it] in, in

IV.2

10 LORDS] *not in* F
12–13 Then ... bear | This burden] *one line in* F

IV.3

5 *Enter Silvius*] *after* brain (3)
105 oak] old Oake

V.1

55 policy] police

V.2

7 nor her] nor
13–16 (*prose*)] You ... consent. | Let ... I | Inuite ...
followers: | Go ... looke you, | Heere ... *Rosalinde*

V.3

15 PAGES] *not in* F
18 ring] *rang*
33–8 And therefore ... spring] *follows first stanza* (15–20)

V.4

111 her hand] *his hand*
112 her bosom] *his bosome*
117–18 If ... true, | Why ... adieu] *one line in* F
161 them] him

2

The following emendations of F are plausible enough or popular
enough to be worthy of record although they have not been
accepted here. The F reading is given first, as modernized in this
edition. There have been many other emendations (those of the
earlier editions are listed in the New Variorum edition).

I.2

  3 would you yet were merrier.] would you yet I were merrier?

 87 the Beu] le Beau

155 them] her

232 all promise] promise

261 taller] shorter (*Rowe*); smaller (*Malone*); lesser (*Spedding*)

I.3

 11 child's father] father's child

 24 try] cry

135 in we] we in

II.1

  5 not] but

 50 friend] friends

II.3

 58 meed] need

II.4

 71 travail] travel

II.7

 73 weary] wearer's

III.2

101 Wintered] Winter

151 Jupiter] pulpiter

III.3

 19 may] it may

 46 horn-beasts] horned beasts

III.4

 14 cast] chaste

 27 lover] a lover

IV.1

124 ROSALIND] CELIA

IV.2

  7 LORD] AMIENS

IV.3

  8 did bid] bid

 88 sister] forester

156 this] his

V.2

  91 or 93 observance] obedience

V.3

      18 the spring time] spring time

      41 untuneable] untimeable

3

The following are the principal additions to, or alterations of, the stage directions in F. The F reading is given second, in the original spelling.

I.1

     26 *Adam stands aside*] *not in* F

     49 *(threatening him)*] *not in* F

     50 *(seizing him by the throat)*] *not in* F

     59 *(coming forward)*] *not in* F

     88 *Exit Dennis*] *not in* F

I.2

     41 *Enter Touchstone*] *Enter Clowne*

 138, etc. *Duke Frederick*] *Duke (similarly elsewhere)*

    152 *He stands aside*] *not in* F

    199 *Orlando and Charles wrestle*] *Wrastle*

    202 *A shout as Charles is thrown*] *Shout*

    203 *(coming forward)*] *not in* F

    208 *Attendants carry Charles off*] *not in* F

    218 *Exit Duke, with Lords, Le Beau, and Touchstone*] *Exit Duke*

    233 *taking a chain from her neck*] *not in* F

    236 *(To Celia)*] *not in* F

    237 *Rosalind and Celia begin to withdraw*] *not in* F

    245 *(To Orlando)*] *not in* F

         Exeunt Rosalind and Celia] *Exit*

    275 *Exit Le Beau*] *not in* F

I.3

     87 *Exit Duke, with Lords*] *Exit Duke, &c.*

II.1

      0 *dressed like foresters*] *like Forresters*

II.3

      0 *from opposite sides*] not in F

II.4

      0 *Enter . . . Touchstone*] Enter Rosaline for Ganimed, Celia
         for Aliena, and Clowne, alias Touchstone

II.5

     35 ALL TOGETHER (*sing*)] *Song. Altogether heere*

II.6

      8 (*Raising him*)] not in F

II.7

      0 *Enter . . . outlaws*] Enter Duke Sen. & Lord, like Out-
         lawes
   136 *Exit*] not in F

III.2

     10 *and Touchstone*] & Clowne
   158 *Exit Touchstone, with Corin*] Exit
   245 *Celia and Rosalind stand back*] not in F
   286 *Exit Jaques*] not in F
   287 (*to Celia*)] not in F

III.3

      0 *Enter Touchstone and Audrey, followed by Jaques*] Enter
         Clowne, Audrey, & Iaques:
 8, 29, 42 (*aside*)] not in F
    66 (*coming forward*)] not in F
    96 (*aside*)] not in F

III.5

      7 (*unobserved*)] not in F
    35 (*coming forward*)] not in F
    66 (*to Phebe*)] not in F
    67 (*to Silvius*)] not in F
    69 (*To Phebe*)] not in F
    74 (*To Silvius*)] not in F
    80 *Exit Rosalind, with Celia and Corin*] Exit

IV.1

    28 (*Going*)] not in F
    29 (*as he goes*)] not in F

IV.2

      0 *Enter Jaques, and Lords dressed as foresters*] Enter Iaques
         and Lords, Forresters

IV.3

     8 *He gives Rosalind a letter, which she reads] not in* F

   157 *Rosalind faints] not in* F

V.1

     0 *Touchstone and Audrey] Clowne and Awdrie*

V.2

   18 *Exit] not in* F

 98–113 *(to Rosalind) etc.] These (nine) stage directions are not in* F

V.3

     0 *Touchstone] Clowne*

V.4

  6–16 *(To the Duke) etc.] These (four) stage directions are not in* F

   33 *Touchstone] Clowne*

  104 *Enter . . . themselves] Enter Hymen, Rosalind, and Celia.*

 113–46 *(to the Duke) etc.] These (ten) stage directions are not in* F

  147 *Second Brother, Jaques de Boys] Second Brother*

 183–8 *(To the Duke) etc.] These (five) stage directions are not in* F

  195 *Exeunt all except Rosalind] Exit*

The Songs

There are no early settings of 'Under the greenwood tree' (II.5) or 'Blow, blow, thou winter wind' (II.7). 'O sweet Oliver', from which Touchstone sings fragments (III.3), appears to have been sung to the tune of 'In peascod time', also known as 'The hunt is up'. The version printed below adapts Touchstone's words to the tune.

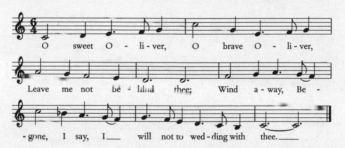

The earliest known setting of 'What shall he have that killed the deer?' (IV.2) is in an arrangement as a catch for four voices made by John Hilton (1599–1657), not published till 1672. The tune may be related to that sung in early performances of the play or it may have been independently composed. It is printed in John H. Long's *Shakespeare's Use of Music* (1955), p. 151.

Thomas Morley's well-known setting of 'It was a lover and his lass' (V.3) appeared in his *First Book of Airs, or Little Short Songs* (1600). Its relation to the play is discussed in the Commentary to V.3.15–38. The version given below is from E. H. Fellowes's edition of Morley's book (1932). The accompaniment is an exact transcription for piano of the lute tablature.

It was a lov-er and his lass, With a hey, with a ho, and a hey no-ni-no, and a hey_____ no-ni no-ni-no, That o'er the green corn-fields did pass, In spring time, in spring time, in spring time, the

ding a ding a ding,   hey   ding a ding a ding,   hey

ding a ding a ding, Sweet   lov - ers love   the spring.

2

Between the acres of the rye,
    With a hey, with a ho, and a hey nonino,
These pretty country fools would lie,
    In spring time, the only pretty ring time,
When birds do sing, hey ding a ding a ding,
Sweet lovers love the spring.

3

This carol they began that hour,
    With a hey, with a ho, and a hey nonino,
How that a life was but a flower,
    In spring time, the only pretty ring time,
When birds do sing, hey ding a ding a ding,
Sweet lovers love the spring.

4

Then pretty lovers take the time,
    With a hey, with a ho, and a hey nonino,
For love is crowned with the prime,
    In spring time, the only pretty ring time,
When birds do sing, hey ding a ding a ding,
Sweet lovers love the spring.

Commentary

In the following pages no attempt has been made to 'explain'
characteristics of Elizabethan syntax that present no difficulties
in comprehension. Accordingly there are no separate notes on,
for example, the so-called third-person plural in '-s' (*the Destinies
decrees*), the 'attraction' of the verb to the nearer subject (*thou
and I am*), the double negatives, the subjunctives, or such
constructions as *better than him I am before knows me*. These are
all described in E. A. Abbott's *A Shakespearian Grammar*, which,
even if in some ways old-fashioned (it was first published in
1869), is still extremely helpful; and in G. L. Brook, *The Language
of Shakespeare* (1976).

Throughout the Commentary the abbreviation F is used for
the first Folio of 1623, in which the play was first published (see
An Account of the Text). Biblical references are to the Bishops'
Bible (1568, etc.), the official English translation of Elizabeth's
reign.

The Characters in the Play: This list is not in F. For comment
on the two characters named Jaques, see Introduction, p. xlix.
That *Jaques* was almost certainly two syllables (pronounced
'Jak-es' or, more probably, 'Jake-wes', in either case with a pun
on 'jakes') is suggested by lines like *The melancholy Jaques grieves
at that* or (from Robert Greene's *Friar Bacon and Friar Bungay*
(1594)) 'Whose surname is Don Jaques Vandermast' and 'Bestir
thee, Jaques, take not now the foil'. Jaques was also an English
family name, as was de Boys.

As You Like It is one of the few Shakespeare texts fully divided

in the original editions into acts and scenes (the formula used in
F being *Actus primus. Scæna Prima*, etc.). Since it is improbable
that such divisions were observed on the Elizabethan public stage
where, except perhaps for one interval, the action seems to have
been continuous, the text of this play may have been specially
prepared for publication.

I.I

2 *but poor a thousand*: A mere (or, in modern idiom, a
'miserable') thousand. Cf. *a many* at 109.

3 *charged*: It was charged, order was given to.
on his blessing: As a condition of obtaining, or retaining,
his (our father's) blessing.

4 *breed*: Raise, educate.

5 *school*: (Probably) university.

6 *his profit*: His progress, the way in which he benefits.

7 *stays*: Retains (or 'detains').

11 *fair with*: Healthy as a result of.
manage: This was the technical term for the training
of a horse in its paces, particularly for military purposes
(from French '*manège*', itself now used as an English
word).

16 *countenance*: Demeanour, bearing; or style of living (as
allowed to Orlando).

17 *hinds*: Servants, farm labourers.
bars me: Excludes me from.

18–19 *as much as in him lies, mines my gentility with my education*: To the best of his ability undermines the advan-
tages I have from my gentle birth, by the poor kind of
education he allows me.

26 *shake me up*: Abuse me violently.

27 *make*: Do (but Orlando's reply involves a pun on the
word).

30 *Marry*: By Mary (with a pun on *mar*, just used by
Oliver).

33–4 *be naught a while*: Leave me, 'make yourself scarce',
or (possibly) be quiet.

36 *prodigal portion*: (With reference to the parable of the
prodigal son, Luke 15:11 ff., and particularly 15–17).

39 *orchard*: The commonest Elizabethan meaning was 'garden', although sometimes the distinction was drawn between orchard and garden.

42–3 *in the gentle condition of blood*: If your behaviour was what that of a brother, of gentle blood, should be.

48 *nearer to his reverence*: More worthy of the respect due to him (the father), because as eldest son 'closest' to him in blood. Oliver's anger is more convincingly explained by Orlando's tone than by anything in the single phrase.

49, 50 *threatening him; seizing him by the throat*: These stage directions are not in F, but the action is made clear by 56–7.

49 *boy*: The word is suggested by Orlando's being younger but was a general term of contempt. Cf. Coriolanus's anger when it is used of him, V.6.101–17, and *Romeo and Juliet*, III.1.65 and 130.

51 *young*: Inexperienced, immature. Perhaps there is also a pun on *elder* in the previous line: the elder tree, associated with Judas, may have had connotations of unreliability and deceit.

52 *villain*: Orlando chooses to take the word in its other sense of 'serf' (our 'villein'). His and Oliver's use for the first time of the contemptuous second-person singular indicates that the quarrel has become ill-tempered.

65 *qualities*: In addition to its modern senses, the word could mean 'accomplishments', 'occupations', 'ranks'.

67 *exercises*: Employments, occupations.

68 *allottery*: Allocation, share.

72 *will*: (1) Desire; (2) portion from the will or testament.

80 *grow upon me*: (Probably another quibble) grow up too fast for my liking; take liberties with me; grow rank (hence *rankness* at 81).

81 *physic*: Cure (by a dose of physic), correct.

103–4 *to stay*: If forced to stay.

111–12 *fleet the time carelessly as they did in the golden world*: While away the time in a carefree way as men did in the Golden Age. *fleet* is normally an intransitive verb,

meaning to 'float', 'pass quickly' or 'glide away';
Shakespeare perhaps invents this use of it to mean
'cause to pass quickly'.

120 *shall*: Must, will need to.

121 *tender*: Undeveloped.

122 *foil*: This may mean only 'defeat', but the noun was
also a technical term used in wrestling for a successful
throwing of the opponent that yet did not result in a
formal 'fall'; *foil* is used again thus at II.2.14.

124 *withal*: With it.

125 *brook*: Endure.

131 *underhand*: Secret, unobtrusive. The derogatory implication was not yet inevitable. (Cf. *natural* at 135.)

134 *an envious emulator of*: One who hates and is jealous
of.

139 *grace himself on thee*: Gain honour at your expense by
defeating you.
     practise: Plot.

145 *anatomize*: Dissect (in the surgical sense, and so it came
to mean 'analyse' and 'reveal').

149–50 *go alone*: Walk without a support (he will be crippled
and will need a crutch).

153 *gamester*: Athlete (but often with derogatory, sometimes with favourable, connotations – like Synge's, and
indeed the frequent Irish, use of 'playboy').

156 *device*: Perhaps this means here 'aspiration' rather than
'invention' or 'manner of thinking'.
     sorts: Classes.
     enchantingly: As if by a real process of enchanting or
bewitching.

159 *misprized*: Despised or (possibly) underrated.

160 *clear all*: Solve all problems.

I.2

1 *coz*: An abbreviation of 'cousin' (which itself could be
used of any relative, as the Duke later at I.3.40 uses
it to Rosalind) but here and throughout the play probably used rather as a term of affection than strictly of
the blood relationship of Rosalind and Celia.

3 *would you yet were*: The emendation to 'would you yet

I were' turns the phrase into a question 'do you want me to be even merrier than that?'; the F text, preserved here, means 'I wish you at least were merrier, whatever be my feelings'.

5 *learn*: Teach (not then only a dialectal or 'incorrect' use).

9 *so*: Provided that.

12 *righteously tempered*: Correctly compounded, blended (an unusual sense of 'righteous').

16 *nor none*: Double negative is common in Shakespeare and does not even necessarily imply emphatic statement. Cf. 26.

18–19 *perforce*: Forcibly.

19 *render*: Give back to.

27–8 *than with safety of a pure blush thou mayst in honour come off again*: Than will enable you to come out of the affair (or escape) with your honour safe and at no more expense than a pure blush (not the blush of shame).

30 *housewife*: This is used here as a half-derogatory term: the goddess Fortune, turning her wheel (the symbol of chance, inconstancy), is compared with a mere housewife, spinning. Cf. 'Dame Fortune'.

37 *honest*: Chaste.

39–40 *Fortune's office to Nature's*: Some commentators place great stress on this conventional contrast between Nature (responsible for beauty and such lasting gifts as intelligence or *wit*) and Fortune (responsible for wealth and position, which can easily be changed), and elevate it into the major 'theme' of the play; the usurper's court is even equated with Fortune, the Forest of Arden with Nature. Shakespeare has other, subtler, things to say.

41 *Enter Touchstone*: The F stage direction is *Enter Clowne*, and Shakespeare may have intended *Touchstone* to be only the name that the clown adopts in the forest. See note on 52 below.

44 *flout*: Mock.

47 *Nature's natural*: One who by nature is deficient in

intelligence: the 'natural' as opposed to the professional fool. Touchstone, however, immediately assumes the role of the latter and Celia is presumably jesting at his expense.

52 *whetstone*: Although the whetstone (for sharpening tools) is not the same as a touchstone (for testing metals), the jest has more point if Celia (or Shakespeare) already thinks of Touchstone as the clown's name.

53–4 *How now, wit, whither wander you*: 'Wit, whither wilt?' was proverbial, addressed to one who was romancing; and there is a further pun on the 'wandering' of the clown's 'wit'.

57 *messenger*: Used not only of one bringing a message but also of the official employed to arrest a state prisoner.

62 *pancakes*: Meat-cakes, fritters.

63 *naught*: Worthless.

   stand to it: Swear to it, justify the statement that. Of these passages of wit, Shaw complained 'Who would endure such humor from any one but Shakespeare? – an Eskimo would demand his money back if a modern author offered him such fare.'

79–81 *My father's love ... these days*: F gives these lines to Rosalind. The F compositor who set these lines (Compositor 'B') made similar errors with other speech-prefixes in V.1 (on R6^v of F), but they were discovered during proofreading and corrected; and another of the compositors ('D') made similar errors in II.3 (on Q5^v) that were not corrected until the second Folio years later. See also An Account of the Text.

80 *taxation*: Criticism, satire. The theory that a secondary meaning is involved, because the Latin 'tax' means 'the sound of a whip stroke', is not fully convincing.

84–6 *since the little wit ... a great show*: For the possible topical allusion, see Introduction, p. xxxiii.

87 *the Beu*: The F reading is preserved here (most editors emend to 'Le Beau') on the assumption that Celia is mocking Le Beau and his mincing speech. (The F spelling *Boon-iour* at 93 perhaps has the same in-

tention.) Only in the following stage direction, however, is the name ever spelt *Beau* in F; elsewhere it
is *Beu*.

89 *put on us*: Force on us, ram down our throats. Possibly
Celia purses her lips in mimicry of Le Beau to make
the point clearer.

92 *the more marketable*: More easily sold, at a profit,
because our weights will have been increased.

95 *colour*: Type, kind (a normal Elizabethan meaning, but
Le Beau's reply perhaps suggests that he is incapable
of understanding it).

98 *Or as the Destinies decrees*: Touchstone, here and in
100, is also aping Le Beau and is deliberately pompous:
hence Celia's reply.

100 *rank*: The *adjective* can mean 'offensively strong in
smell', a meaning that Rosalind seizes on.

102 *amaze*: Bewilder.

106–7 *yet to do*: Still to come.

109 *Well, the beginning that is dead and buried*: This has
often been taken as a question but may be a cynical
comment on Le Beau's obvious delight in making much
of what is already past.

112 *proper*: Handsome.

114 *bills*: Notices, proclamations (such as are sometimes
carried on the back, slung from the neck). Conceivably
there is a pun on *bills* meaning 'halberds'. Le Beau's
over-formal language reminds Rosalind of legal jargon
and she replies with a legal phrase and a pun on *presence* ('presents', legal documents).

118 *that*: So that.

121 *dole*: Lamentation.

131–2 *broken music*: The usual meaning, 'part music', hardly
makes sense here. The gloss 'broken instruments' (with
broken ribs or frets) is better than this (or than 'broken
consort').

138 *Flourish*: A fanfare of horns or trumpets (normally to
mark the entrance of a king, queen or other ruler).

140 *forwardness*: Rashness.

148 *such odds in the man*: So marked a superiority in the

man (Charles), so much in the man's favour (as against
the youth).

163 *with your eyes*: Clearly, as you really are.

168–9 *therefore be misprized*: Be condemned, or undervalued,
on that account.

172 *wherein*: In a matter in which.

175 *gracious*: Graced, lucky enough to enjoy favour (including the favours of Fortune).

184 *deceived*: Mistaken (through underestimating your
strength).

190 *working*: Aim.

196 *come your ways*: Come on.

197 *be thy speed*: Speed thee, grant thee success.

205 *breathed*: Exercised. The modern idiom is 'have not
yet warmed up'.

214 *still*: Always.

220–22 *I am more proud to be Sir Rowland's son, . . . to Frederick*:
Perhaps these words are spoken, in defiance, as the
Duke leaves the stage.

221 *calling*: Station in life (rather than 'title', a meaning
for which there is no recorded authority).

230 *Sticks me at heart*: Pierces (me in) my heart.

232 *justly*: Precisely.

233 *taking a chain from her neck*: The warrant for this addition to F is III.2.175.

234 *out of suits with*: Dismissed from the favour of (and
therefore, like a dismissed servant, deprived of the
'suit' or livery).

240 *quintain*: The post, block or perhaps figure used for
tilting practice.

242 *would*: Wishes.

245 *Have with you*: I am coming with you.

247 *urged conference*: Invited conversation.

249 *Or*: Either.

253 *condition*: Temper or mood.

254 *misconsters*: Misconstrues (a variant form, with the
accent on the second syllable).

255 *humorous*: The victim of a disproportion of the four
'humours' (which had to be in perfect balance in a

man's make-up if he was to be normal).

264 *whose*: The general sense, not any particular word, provides the antecedent for *whose*, which refers to both the daughters just mentioned.

268 *argument*: Line of reasoning.

273 *in a better world than this*: If we should meet in happier circumstances.

275 *bounden*: Indebted.

276 *smother*: The dense and more suffocating smoke of the smouldering fire. The corresponding modern idiom is 'out of the frying pan into the fire'.

278 *Rosalind*: Here, and in the first stage direction and the text of I.3, F has *Rosaline*. It is often difficult in Elizabethan ('secretary') handwriting to distinguish between 'e' and 'd'; but *Rosaline* and *Rosalind* may only be alternative forms of the one name. Rosaline is the heroine of *Love's Labour's Lost*, and Romeo's first love was Rosaline. The verses of Orlando and Touchstone in III.2 show that 'Rosalind' is the heroine's 'real' name here – though pronounced, or jocularly mispronounced, to rhyme with 'lined'.

I.3

14 *trodden paths*: Perhaps Celia is implying that she and Rosalind were unconventional in speaking as they did to Orlando after the wrestling.

18 *Hem*: This is a pun on the two senses, the one from sewing, the other imitating the sound of a cough; it is suggested by *burs* ('bur' could also refer to a choking sensation in the throat).

19–20 *cry 'hem' and have him*: This time the pun is on *hem* and *him*. Some commentators have thought the phrase proverbial but it is not listed in the usual source books.

24 *try*: Try a bout or wrestling match (with Orlando – with the usual sexual pun on *fall*).

31 *chase*: Pursuit, sequence (another pun, from hunting).

32 *dearly*: Intensely.

39 *your safest haste*: All speed possible, in the interests of your own safety.

40 *cousin*: Niece.

47 *frantic*: Out of my senses.

51 *purgation*: In addition to the medical meaning, the word was used in theology (both of the purification of the soul in Purgatory and of the declaration of innocence on oath) and as a legal term, of the proving of innocence, particularly by ordeal. Cf. V.4.42–3.

60 *friends*: Apparently used in the now obsolete sense, 'relatives'.

61 *What's that to me*: How is that relevant to me?

65 *stayed*: Retained, kept.

68 *remorse*: The word already had its modern meaning of 'compunction' or 'repentance', but also commonly meant 'compassion'.

71 *still*: Always, constantly.

73 *Juno's swans*: The author of the anonymous play *Soliman and Perseda* (possibly Kyd) also refers to 'Juno's goodly swans | Or Venus' milk-white doves', although most Elizabethans knew and accepted the classical tradition that the swans were Venus' birds (Juno's being peacocks). The 'explanation' that Shakespeare is transferring the symbolic qualities of Venus, goddess of love, to Juno, goddess of marriage (and 'patroness' of this play), seems strained and somewhat desperate.

81 *doom*: Judgement, sentence.

102 *now at our sorrows pale*: Now pale or overcast in sympathy with our sorrows.

110 *umber*: Yellow-coloured earth (so named from Umbria, in Italy). The point is that Elizabethan ladies of degree took care to protect their complexions from the sun, and their paleness would have been in marked contrast to the complexions of country women.

111 *pass along*: Go on our way.

113 *more than common tall*: This contradicts I.2.261, which is almost certainly 'wrong'.

114 *suit me all points*: Dress and equip myself in all ways.

115 *curtle-axe*: Short sword. This form of the noun 'coutelas' (our 'cutlass') arose by mistaken etymology.

118 *swashing*: Swaggering. The word (or its variant

'washing') was used also of a blow in fencing, as in *Romeo and Juliet*, I.1.61–2: 'Gregory, remember thy washing blow.'

outside: Perhaps, but not necessarily, in the tailoring sense (as contrasted with the lining). Similarly, *outface* at 120 perhaps contains a pun on the tailoring sense of 'face', meaning 'trim'.

119 *mannish*: Masculine.

120 *outface it with their semblances*: Bluff it out (the 'indefinite *it*'), relying on their mere appearance of strength.

126 *Aliena*: The stranger, or one who is 'not herself'. The accentuation is in doubt, but a stress on the second syllable seems possible in this line.

127 *assayed*: Attempted.

131 *woo*: Win over, persuade.

II.1

0 *like foresters*: (Probably) in 'Kentish green'.

4 *envious*: Given to enmity or hatred.

5 *the penalty of Adam*: According to the traditional view, in Eden there was perpetual spring; the change of seasons, with the hardships of winter, was a consequence of Adam's fall. Apparently, the Duke asks a third question, 'Do we not feel?', and goes on to imply that it is nevertheless a good thing so to feel, for the reasons he gives.

11 *feelingly*: By making themselves felt.

12 *uses of*: Perhaps both 'ways of life associated with' and 'profits to be had from'.

13–14 *the toad ... head*: Two superstitions of natural history are alluded to here: that the toad was poisonous, and that it had a precious stone (alternatively, a bone) in its head that had magical properties and was an antidote against poison.

15 *exempt from public haunt*: Not exposed to, or visited by, people generally.

18 *I would not change it*: Some editors unnecessarily transfer these words to the Duke. As Furness said, 'The Duke has asked a question. Is no one to answer?'

22 *fools*: This means 'simple creatures', not 'idiots'. Cf. 40.

23 *burghers*: Citizens, of the woods, their own territories (*confines*).

24 *forkèd heads*: Barbed arrows.

27 *kind*: Respect.

31 *antick*: Possibly only 'old' (our 'antique'), but possibly 'antic' in the sense of 'contorted', 'queerly shaped'. The word is to be stressed on the first syllable.

33 *sequestered*: Separated.

41 *of*: By.

44 *moralize*: Draw morals from, or explicate.

46 *needless*: Unneeding (the stream had water enough already).

50 *of*: By.

   velvet friend: *velvet* must refer to the coat of the deer, although it is also the technical term for the covering of the developing horns of a stag; *friend* has been altered by some editors to 'friends'. In any case, it is the deer that is abandoned, not Jaques; the pronouns create some confusion throughout this speech.

51–2 *part . . . The flux*: Separate (or 'separate the miserable one *from*') the flood. The phrase may be basically proverbial.

52 *careless*: Carefree.

58 *invectively*: Vehemently.

61 *and what's worse*: And everything that is even worse.

67 *cope*: Encounter and engage with (in combat or debate).

II.2

3 *Are of consent and sufferance in*: Have agreed and been accessory to.

8 *roynish*: Scurvy.

13 *wrestler*: Probably three syllables.

17 *that gallant*: Orlando.

19 *suddenly*: Immediately.

20 *quail*: Usually explained as 'slacken' but may well retain its usual meaning of 'cower', 'shrink back because afraid'.

II.3

3 *memory*: Memorial.

4 *make you*: Are you doing.

7 *so fond to*: So foolish as to.

8 *bonny prizer*: Big (or strong) prize-fighter.

15 *Envenoms*: Poisons; but Adam seems to mean that Orlando's bravery has led people like the Duke to treat him as if he were poisonous or dangerous. There is probably a reference to the poisoned garment that Deianira was tricked into giving to Hercules. (The story is told by Ovid in the *Metamorphoses* IX, 138 ff.).

23 *use*: Are accustomed.

26 *practices*: Plots.

27 *place*: Dwelling, home. (Shakespeare's own house in Stratford was called 'New Place'.)

30 *so*: Provided that.

32 *boisterous*: Violent.
   enforce: Gain by force.

37 *diverted blood*: A relationship turned away from its natural course (perhaps a kind of pun, for physicians also 'diverted' real blood).

39 *thrifty hire I saved*: Wages I, thriftily, saved.

42 *thrown*: Lie thrown, or be thrown.

43, 44 *He that doth the ravens feed, . . . the sparrow*: Shakespeare may be thinking of any one of a number of biblical passages (for example, Psalms 147:9, Matthew 10:29, Luke 12:6–7). Cf. Hamlet's 'there is special providence in the fall of a sparrow' (V.2.213–14).

47 *lusty*: Vigorous (*not* 'lustful').

49 *rebellious*: (Probably) causing rebellion (in the body).

53 *kindly*: This means either 'beneficial' or '(only insofar) as it ought to be in the ordinary course of nature'.

57 *antique*: Ancient, former. This is perhaps not the same word as *antick* at II.1.31, although the variation in the F spellings – *anticke*, *antique* – may be due merely to the two different compositors ('C' and 'D') who set up the sections.

58 *sweat*: The past tense.
   meed: Reward. Furness recorded that his copy of F read 'neede', which also makes good sense; but inspection reveals that somebody (probably a previous owner) had altered the word by erasing a minim.

61 *choke their service up*: This somewhat unusual phrase
probably has a biblical origin, in Matthew 13:22: 'the
care of this world, and the deceitfulness of riches,
choke up the word', where a gardening metaphor is
being used. The meaning would thus be that the serv-
ices are choked out of existence by the promotion
gained. Another gardening metaphor follows at 63–5.

65 *lieu of*: Return for.

68 *low*: Humble.

69 *thee*: This is the first time Adam presumes to use the
familiar form.

71 *seventeen*: F's *seauentie* is an obvious slip, for it has
seauenteene at 73.

74 *a week*: The modern idiom is 'in the day'. Alternatively
the phrase may mean, in ironic understatement, 'too
late by a week'.

II.4

1 *weary*: F's *merry* must be an error (perhaps the manuscript read 'wery'). Rosalind can hardly be pretending
to be merry, to encourage Celia, for Touchstone seems
to catch up the word *weary* in his reply.

6 *weaker vessel*: The phrase is, of course, biblical (1 Peter
3:7), and indeed Rosalind's following words are a kind
of jocular paraphrase of that verse.
doublet-and-hose: Jacket and knee-breeches (normal
Elizabethan male dress).

10 *no cross*: A pun and not an original one: (1) no trouble;
(2) no coin (some coins had a cross on one side). There
may, however, be a further pun on Matthew 10:38 ('And
he that taketh not his cross, and followeth, is not worthy
of me') or the comparable Luke 14:27.

16–17 *Ay, be so . . . solemn talk*: The lines are printed as prose
in F but (if *Ay* is treated as extrametrical, in the normal
way) make good verse. They mark the modulation to
the verse of the Corin–Silvius exchange, and
Rosalind's lines 40–41 modulate from that verse back
to Touchstone's prose.

27 *fantasy*: Fancy, affection (not used pejoratively).

34 *Wearing*: Perhaps this was a variant of 'wearying';

perhaps it was a Shakespearian, or Warwickshire, spelling of 'wearying'; more probably it *means* 'wearing (out)'.

40 *searching of*: (In) probing (a medical term).

41 *hard adventure*: Painful experience.

45 *batler*: The wooden club used for beating clothes in the process of washing them.

46 *chopt*: Chapped.

47 *peascod*: The peascod or pea-pod was associated with several rustic superstitions in connection with wooing and was an appropriate 'lucky' gift. No doubt there are the usual quibbles throughout this passage on 'peas', 'cods' (compare 'codpiece') and possibly 'sword' and 'stone'.

51 *mortal in folly*: Foolish as only a mortal can be – unless it means 'mortally, extremely, foolish' (but that would seem to be a later use). Perhaps Rosalind takes *mortal* in the sense of 'fatal'.

52, 53 *ware*: Another pun: (1) aware; (2) wary, frightened.

53 *Nay*: Indeed (not implying contradiction).

55–6 *passion . . . fashion*: The rhyme suggests that Rosalind is parodying Silvius's style; see Introduction, p. xxv.

57 *something*: Somewhat.

69 *entertainment*: Provision for the needs of a guest.

78 *recks to find*: Cares about finding. (F's *wreakes* probably signifies only a different pronunciation.) In lines 77–9 Shakespeare may be thinking of the story of Nabal in 1 Samuel 25.

80 *cote*: Cottage.
bounds of feed: Full extent of his pastures.

81 *on sale*: In the process of being sold (as 85–7 make clear).

84 *in my voice*: So far as my voice or decision is concerned.

85 *What*: Who.

86 *but erewhile*: Only a short time ago.

88 *stand with honesty*: Is not inconsistent with fair dealing.

90 *to pay for it*: Something with which to pay for it.

91 *mend*: Amend, improve.

92 *waste*: Pass.

94 *upon report*: After hearing details.

96 *feeder*: Servant.

II.5

0 *others*: In stage practice, usually a group of attendant lords.

1 *AMIENS*: F has the simple heading *Song* but the following dialogue leaves no doubt that Amiens is the singer.

3 *turn*: Adapt.

14 *ragged*: Hoarse.

19–20 *I care not for their names, they owe me nothing*: This is normally taken as a quibble on *names*, in the sense of signatures on a legal document acknowledging a debt.

23 *that*: That which.

24 *dog-apes*: Dog-faced baboons.

26 *beggarly*: To be expected from a beggar.

28 *cover the while*: In the meantime lay the covers (the utensils for a meal), 'set the table'.

30 *look you*: Seek you, look for you (not an error but a regular transitive use of the verb).

32 *disputable*: Argumentative, disputatious.

36 *to live i'th'sun*: To live the free, irresponsible life of nature.

43 *note*: Melody.

44 *in despite of my invention*: To spite my (lack of) inventiveness, to prove that 'invention' isn't necessary for the composition of nonsense.

46 *JAQUES*: F heads this speech also *Amy.* (Amiens) – but he can hardly have three consecutive speeches. It would be possible for Jaques to say only *Thus it goes*, handing Amiens a sheet of paper, and for Amiens both to sing Jaques's words and to ask about *ducdame*.

51 *Ducdame*: 'Explanations' range from a Latin phrase to an Italian to a Welsh to a Romany (all of course slightly adjusted) but Jaques gives the best explanation: the word is deliberate nonsense, which will incite fools to form a circle ('go into a huddle'!).

54 *An if*: If.

56 *Greek*: Meaningless ('it's all Greek to me').

58 *first-born of Egypt*: The words are, of course, from
Exodus 11:5 and 12:12 and 29, but their relevance is
not obvious, even if Jaques is comparing the Duke's
banishment with the journey of the Israelites into the
wilderness after the first-born of Egypt had been slain
by the Lord.

59 *banquet*: This is probably used in the alternative sense
of a light meal, particularly of fruit etc. The meal may
have been laid out in the inner stage, if any, or at the
rear or side of the stage; no Elizabethan audience would
have been worried that Orlando and Adam do not see
it in the next 'scene'.

II.6

5 *comfort*: Comfort thyself, take comfort.
6 *uncouth*: Unknown, or wild, desolate.
7 *conceit*: Imagination.
9 *comfortable*: Comforted, of good comfort.
10 *presently*: Immediately.
13 *Well said*: Well done!
cheerly: Cheerful. F's *cheerely* may conceivably be
'cheerily'.

II.7

0 *Enter Duke Senior, Amiens . . . outlaws*: F has *Enter Duke
Sen. & Lord, like Out-lawes*. One assumes that *Lords*
is intended, and that they include Amiens, who went
off to find the Duke at the end of II.5 and who, as the
singer of the company, presumably sings *Blow, blow,
thou winter wind*. But though the Duke says *Give us
some music and, good cousin, sing*, the song is simply
headed *Song*, with no name, so that all this is mere
inference. It is improbable that *like Out-lawes* here
points to a different costume from the *like Forresters*
of II.1.

3 *but even now*: Only a moment ago.
5 *compact of jars*: Made up of discords.
6 *discord in the spheres*: This alludes to the Pythagorean
belief, beautifully expounded in *The Merchant of Venice*,
V.1.60 ff.: 'There's not the smallest orb which thou
beholdest | But in his motion like an angel sings . . .',

the notes of the individual planets, or of their spheres, combining to form the heavenly 'harmony'. Such harmony was one of the basic principles of the universe – and would need to be reversed before Jaques could become *musical*.

13 *motley*: Leslie Hotson has argued that the motley of the Elizabethan fool, including the professional fool, was not, as modern directors believe, breeches and hose quartered like racing colours, but the long robe or petticoat, made of cloth woven from threads of mixed colours, and most often basically green or brown. Alternatively, each robe may have had a small design woven in colour.
    a miserable world: Emendation of this natural parenthesis to 'ah' or 'word' is hardly necessary, even on the theory that *world* is a variant Elizabethan spelling of 'word'.

19 *'Call me not fool till heaven hath sent me fortune'*: A development of the proverbial 'fortune favours fools'.

20 *dial*: Either a watch or the common pocket sundial.
    poke: Pocket, wallet or bag. Hotson sees a reference to a standard joke that the fool's coat was itself his cloakbag, in which he could conveniently be carried off.

28 *And thereby hangs a tale*: And more could be said. (The phrase was a cliché.) Some critics have read this passage to mean that Touchstone was parodying Jaques, who does not see that the joke is on him, but there is no good reason for thinking so. What is quite likely is that Jaques is enjoying indecent puns by Touchstone on *hour* (pronounced like 'whore') and 'tail'.

29 *moral*: Perhaps a verb ('moralize'), more probably an adjective ('moralistic').

30 *Chanticleer*: The cock in the traditional story of Reynard the Fox.

32 *sans intermission*: Without pause. *intermission* is to be pronounced as five syllables, and *sans* probably as if it were an English word.

39 *dry as the remainder biscuit*: The brain of an idiot was thought to be hard and dry; and nothing could be harder than would have been the seamen's biscuits left over after a long Elizabethan voyage. Cf. III.2. 190–91.

40 *places*: Perhaps a kind of pun, with the second meaning of 'extracts', quotations learned off by heart.

41 *observation*: Again five syllables, and probably has the older sense of 'maxim' or 'comment'.

44 *suit*: Another pun: (1) petition; (2) clothing; and this in turn suggests the pun in the next line on *weed*. This is one of the image sequences that occur several times in Shakespeare's plays. (It was first noticed by Walter Whiter.)

52 *why ... way*: Perhaps another atrocious pun.

53–5 *He that a fool doth very wisely hit ... of the bob*: If Theobald's emendation of F is adopted (the addition of *Not to* to 55, to complete both metre and sense), the lines mean: 'a man on whom a fool, in his fool's wisdom, scores a hit, is very foolish – even if he smarts under the criticism – if he does not pretend to be insensible of it'. Other bare possibilities are to punctuate 'Doth, very foolishly although he smart, | Seem ...' or to explain 'the *wise* man appears to be foolish *and to be* insensitive'.

55 *bob*: 'Bitter jest', 'gibe'; may also be used metaphorically: 'rap over the fingers'.

56 *unatomized*: Dissected.

57 *squandering glances*: Random hits.

58–61 *Invest me in my motley ... my medicine*: These are the lines, together with 47–9 and 70–87, that have been thought by some to allude to Ben Jonson. Jonson's boast in the Induction to *Every Man out of his Humour* (1599), 'With an armèd and resolvèd hand, | I'll strip the raggèd follies of the time | Naked as at their birth', is certainly similar in tone. There are other parallels not only in Jonson's work but also in John Marston's. Jaques is, then, speaking in the language of the best satirists of the period, and at 70–87 is making the satirist's usual defence of his satire.

63 *for a counter*: In exchange for a mere imitation coin (which I will give you for telling me).

66 *sting*: Sexual lust.

67 *embossèd*: Protuberant.

headed: Having come to a head, like boils (and *evils* may mean 'carbuncles' or 'eruptions of the skin'; the 'King's evil' was scrofula).

68 *caught*: Almost a pun: 'caught' as one catches a cold and as one catches a bur in clothing. Cf. I.3.14–15.

70–87 *Why, who cries . . . who come here*: For the topical relevance of this speech, see note on 58–61 above. The 'incompleteness' of 70 does not point to textual corruption: there are many other such lines in Shakespeare.

73 *Till that the weary very means do ebb*: This is a notorious crux but no satisfactory emendation has been proposed. A meaning can be extracted: 'Until the very means (wealth, on which pride is based), being exhausted, may be said to run out as the tide does.'

76 *cost of*: Wealth needed to maintain.

79 *function*: Office, occupation.

80 *That says his bravery is not on my cost*: Who says his fine clothes are not bought at my expense (that is, tells me to mind my own business and not criticize him). The image link of *bravery* and *suits* is again worthy of note.

82 *mettle*: Substance, spirit.

84 *do him right*: Describes him correctly.

85 *free*: Guiltless.

86 *taxing*: Criticism.

95 *touched my vein*: Diagnosed my motive or state of mind.

97 *inland*: Near the centre of civilization (as opposed to 'country bred').

98 *nurture*: Manners, culture.

101–2 *An you will not be answered with reason, I must die*: The attempt to make these lines scan as verse is misguided: the drop into prose emphasizes the laconic nature of Jaques's reply. It is customary on the stage for him to nibble something as he says these words – an apple, or even a date, grape, or raisin in deference to the editors who have suspected the 'reason'/'raisin' quibble, as in Falstaff's 'If reasons were as plentiful as blackberries' (*Henry IV, Part I*, II.4.235).

103–4 *Your gentleness shall force, . . . to gentleness*: The phrase

is probably proverbial; a similar one has been found
in Publius Syrus's *Sententiae*.

112 *melancholy*: Because they shut out the sunshine.

113 *Lose and neglect*: Pass, without worrying about them.

115 *knolled*: Rung, pealed (but with no implication of
mournfulness).

126 *upon command*: At your will or pleasure.

127 *wanting*: Needs.

133 *weak*: Weakening, causing weakness.

136 *your good comfort*: The goodness and kindness you
have shown.

140–67 *All the world's a stage, . . . sans everything*: On the background to this famous speech, see Introduction, pp.
xxx, xxxiii, xxxvi–xxxviii. There is even a passage in
the old play of *Damon and Pithias* (1564): 'Pythagoras
said, that this world was like a stage, | Whereon many
play their parts.' Shakespeare's originality is in the
development of the idea and in the tone, appropriate
to Jaques.

145 *Mewling*: Not just 'whimpering' (a meaning that may
derive from misunderstanding of this passage) but
'mewing like a cat'.

147 *creeping like snail*: This image may not have come from
Shakespeare's memories of Warwickshire after all,
even if he was thinking of his schooldays, for Nashe
has in *The First Part of Pasquil's Apology* (1590),
speaking of contemporary scholars, 'I wonder how
these silly snails, creeping but yesterday out of shops
and Grammar-schools, dare thrust out their feeble
horns, against so tough and mighty adversaries' (as
their predecessors).

149 *woeful*: Full of woe.

151 *pard*: Panther or leopard.

152 *Jealous in honour*: Quick to take offence in matters
thought to concern his honour.

155 *capon*: Chicken (and 'capon-justice' was the regular
term for one who could be bribed with such a gift).

157 *saws*: Sayings.

modern instances: Trite or commonplace (*not* 'up-to-date') illustrations.

159 *pantaloon*: The dotard of Italian comedy.

161 *hose*: Breeches.

165 *history*: History play, chronicle.

166 *mere*: Complete.

167 *Enter Orlando with Adam*: Capell first recorded the tradition that a contemporary remembered Shakespeare's having played a part, presumably Adam, in which he was carried on to the stage on another's back.

180 *rude*: Rough.

181 *Hey-ho*: This is common in refrains and though spelt *Heigh ho* in F does not necessarily refer to a sigh.
holly: Associated with rejoicing and festivities.

182 *Most friendship . . . mere folly*: Perhaps this too is a proverb.

197 *effigies*: This is an alternative, singular, form of 'effigy' (meaning 'image') and is stressed on the second syllable.

198 *limned*: Portrayed, or reproduced.

III.I

2 *the better part made mercy*: For the greater part so merciful by disposition.

3 *argument*: Subject.

6 *Seek him with candle*: The reference (coming ironically from the Duke) is to Luke 15:8, 'What woman, having ten pieces of silver, if she lose one, doth not light a candle, and sweep the house, and seek diligently till she find it?' (the verse that follows 'joy shall be in heaven over one sinner that repenteth . . .').

7 *turn*: Return.

10 *seize*: Perhaps in the sense of 'seise' (take legal possession of); *extent* at 17 is the legal term for a writ for taking the initial steps in the seising of land as security for debt etc.

11 *quit*: Acquit.
mouth: That is, words, evidence.

16 *of such a nature*: Whose duty it is to do this.

18 *expediently*: In haste, expeditiously.
turn him going: Send him packing.

III.2

1 *Hang there*: No doubt one of the pillars supporting the
'heavens' over the bare Elizabethan public stage would
serve well enough for a tree (Rosalind says later that
she found Orlando's poem *on a tree*). Hanging love
poems (or carving names) on trees was part of the
traditional behaviour of the pastoral lover.

2 *thrice-crownèd*: Diana (Artemis), the goddess of
chastity, was identified with Proserpina (Hecate) in the
underworld and with Luna (Selene) in the sky; alternatively, the passage suggests three functions of Diana:
goddess of the moon (2), of chastity (3) and of the
hunt (4).

4 *Thy huntress' name*: Rosalind is thought of as a nymph
in Diana's train because she too is chaste.
sway: Control.

6 *character*: Inscribe.

10 *unexpressive*: Inexpressible.

15 *naught*: Worthless.

16 *private*: Secluded; not public. (The contrast between
solitary and *private* is none too clear.)

18 *spare*: Frugal.

19 *humour*: Temperament, or mood. (Cf. 'I am not in the
humour.')

23 *wants*: Lacks.

28 *complain of good breeding*: Complain that he has been
denied good upbringing or birth.

30 *natural philosopher*: (1) A philosopher who studies
nature; (2) a foolish pretender to thought.

35–6 *damned . . . on one side*: A comparable modern idiom
is 'half-baked'.

39 *manners*: Another quibble: (1) forms of polite behaviour; (2) morals.

46 *salute*: Greet.
but: Unless.

49 *Instance*: Give an example.

50 *still*: Constantly.
fells: Fleeces.

61 *civet*: The perfume obtained (as Touchstone is quick

to point out) from the *flux* or glandular secretion of the civet cat.

62 *worms' meat*: Food for worms, a mere corpse. (Mercutio in *Romeo and Juliet*, III.1.107, when stabbed, says 'They have made worms' meat of me.')

62–3 *in respect of*: In comparison with.

64 *perpend*: Consider, weigh the facts.

68 *God make incision . . . raw*: Two explanations have been offered: one from surgery (blood-letting to cure soreness or sickness), one from gardening (grafting to improve what is *raw* or wild).

69 *get*: Earn.

71 *content with my harm*: Patient under my misfortunes.

76–7 *bell-wether*: The leading sheep of the flock (obviously here a ram, *not* a castrated male) on whose neck a bell was hung.

84 *Ind*: Indies. It was, often at least, pronounced to rhyme with 'lined'. But the suggestion may be that Orlando is straining for rhymes.

88 *lined*: Drawn (but the word is also used, as Touchstone uses it at 101, of the male dog covering the bitch).

94 *right butter-women's rank to market*: The genuine movement of the butter-women jogging along to the market. Perhaps there is also a picture of the butter-women in a rank or line, at regular intervals, but the later phrase *false gallop* makes it probable that *rank* here means 'pace' or 'jog-trot'. Both phrases may be reminiscences of a passage in Nashe's *Strange News* (1592): 'I would trot a false gallop through the rest of his ragged verses, but that if I should report his rhyme doggerel aright I must make my verses, as he doth his, run hobbling like a brewer's cart upon the stones, and observe no length in their feet.'

99 *kind*: Its own kin or species.

101 *Wintered*: Used in winter.

103–4 *They that reap . . . cart with Rosalind*: Touchstone's parody is far from genteel: 'Those that sow must reap, and so Rosalind must pay the cost of what she has done – by being carted like a prostitute.' Public exposure in, and whipping at the rear of, a cart was the regular punishment.

113 *graff*: Graft (which is a later form of the word). Perhaps there is a pun on *you* and 'yew', and reference to Matthew 7:17–18: '. . . a corrupt tree bringeth forth evil fruit . . .'

114 *medlar*: The tree bearing the apple-like fruit which is fit for eating only when decayed. There is also a pun, of course, on 'meddler': Touchstone is interfering.

114–15 *then it will be the earliest fruit i'th'country*: The fruit of the medlar (which normally bears late in the season) will then be rotten far sooner (and rottenness is the *right virtue* or true merit of the medlar).

121–2 *Why should this . . . unpeopled? No*: Some editors have defended F's *Desert* against Rowe's emendation *a desert*, but Orlando's versification is mostly jingle. F has a comma after *be*, but probably a question is intended: 'Why should this be a desert? Because it is unpeopled? No.' It could be argued, however, that the comma makes slightly better sense of Orlando's lame poem as a whole: 'Why should lack of people make this a desert? I'll put tongues on every tree and solve that difficulty.'

124 *civil sayings*: Maxims appropriate to civilization (as against deserts).

126 *erring*: Wandering (with no sense of error).

127–8 *the stretching of a span . . . sum of age*: A span is the distance measured by thumb and little finger, and Shakespeare is no doubt alluding to Psalm 39:5, 'Behold thou hast made my days as it were an hand breadth long' ('span' in the Prayer Book).

128 *Buckles in*: Encloses.

135 *quintessence*: The quintessence was the fifth 'essence' (additional to the four elements) of which heavenly bodies were thought to be composed and which was latent in everything; astrologers aimed at isolating it by distillation (140), in a search for the secrets of transmutation.
sprite: Spirit.

136 *in little*: In the little world of man, the microcosm, of which every part corresponded to something in the universe, or macrocosm.

137 *Heaven Nature charged*: Heaven gave orders to Nature.

139 *wide-enlarged*: Endowed in fullest measure.

140 *presently*: Immediately.

141 *Helen's cheek*: The beautiful complexion or face of Helen of Troy.

143 *better part*: Probably Atalanta's 'grace' or her 'physique' (since she was such a splendid runner – cf. 268–9), but the meaning is in dispute. Another suggestion is Atalanta's 'determination to remain chaste'.

144 *Sad Lucretia's modesty*: Lucretia killed herself after she was violated by Tarquin.
   Sad: Serious.

146 *synod*: Probably used here in its astrological sense of 'conjunction'.

148 *touches*: Traits.

151 *Jupiter*: The generally accepted emendation to 'pulpiter' (preacher) is gratuitous. Rosalind swears by Jupiter and by Jove in II.2 and is no doubt comparing and contrasting the poet, or Celia who reads his poem, with the not-so-gentle voice of Jupiter speaking from heaven.

154 *How now? Back, friends*: It seems more likely that Celia is telling Corin and Touchstone to stand back than that she puns on 'back-friends' – (1) false friends; (2) people standing behind her back, whom she now sees for the first time.

157–8 *bag and baggage ... scrip and scrippage*: To be allowed to depart with one's bags and their contents was an honourable condition on which to surrender; Touchstone and Corin may have no bags, but Corin has the shepherd's pouch (the *scrip*) and Touchstone, presumably, the fool's wallet. *baggage* already meant also a strumpet (and Touchstone has just made his uncomplimentary comparison of Rosalind with a prostitute) and so *scrippage* (a word he invents for the contents of the scrip) may be better worth having than baggage.

168 *should be*: Came to be.

169 *seven of the nine days*: The phrase depends on the proverbial 'a nine days' wonder'.

171–2 *I was never ... hardly remember*: Rosalind jokingly pretends to accept two wild beliefs: Pythagoras's doctrine of the transmigration of souls, and the Irish superstition that rats could be killed with rhymes used as spells.

172 *that*: In that; when.

173 *Trow you*: Do you know.

178–80 *it is a hard matter ... so encounter*: There is an old proverb: 'Friends may meet but mountains never greet.'

182 *Is it possible*: That is, possible that you don't know.

186 *out of all whooping*: Far beyond what all cries of astonishment can express.

188 *Good my complexion*: Pardon my blushes.

189 *caparisoned*: Dressed, decked out.

190–91 *a South Sea of discovery*: As tedious as a voyage of discovery in the interminable South Seas.

192 *apace*: Rapidly, or immediately.

203 *stay*: Wait for.

207–8 *sad brow and true maid*: With a serious face and on your honour as a virgin.

214 *Wherein went he*: In what clothes was he dressed?

215 *makes he*: Is he doing.

218 *Gargantua*: The giant of fairy tale ('and of Rabelais's famous story).

225 *atomies*: Motes, specks.

225–6 *resolve the propositions of*: Solve the problems put forward for solution by.

227 *relish it with good observance*: Sauce it and make it more palatable, by paying respectful attention.

229 *Jove's tree*: The oak (sacred to Jove).

231 *Give me audience*: Let me do the talking.

233–4 *There lay he ... wounded knight*: Celia is possibly adopting the language of the fashionable romance.

235–6 *well becomes the ground*: Befits the earth (with a quibble on *ground* meaning 'background').

237 *'holla'*: Whoa! The image is carried on in *curvets*: 'leaps about like a frisky horse'.

238 *furnished*: Dressed (as also at V.4.204).

239 *heart*: With a pun on 'hart'.

240 *burden*: The word was used both of the refrain and of the bass or undersong. Cf. IV.2.13 and note.

244 *bring me out*: Put me out.

250 *God buy you*: God be with you (our 'goodbye').

254 *moe*: More. It is not clear why Orlando is given this older form when Jaques uses *more*.

255 *ill-favouredly*: Badly; or with a disapproving expression.

257 *just*: Exactly, quite so.

264–5 *conned them out of rings*: Learned them by heart from rings (in which mottoes were inscribed).

266 *right painted cloth*: In the authentic manner of painted cloth (the cheaper alternative to tapestry), on which were painted scriptural and other texts.

272 *breather*: 'Man alive' in modern idiom.

281 *There I shall see mine own figure*: As Furness said, the line is unworthy of Jaques!

304 *trots hard*: Moves at an uncomfortable jog-trot.

313 *wasteful*: (Perhaps) causing to waste away.

316–17 *go as softly*: Walk as slowly.

319 *stays*: Stands.

327 *cony*: Rabbit.

328 *kindled*: Born.

330 *purchase*: Acquire.
     removed: Remote.

332 *religious uncle*: Uncle who was a member of a religious order. Some editors, implausibly, have suggested some connection between this supposed *religious uncle* and the *old religious man* of V.4.157.

333 *inland*: City, cultured. Cf. II.7.97 and note.
     courtship: (1) Court life; (2) wooing.

336 *touched with*: Stained with; or accused of.

344–5 *I will not cast away … are sick*: There may be an allusion to Matthew 9:12: 'They that be whole need not the physician, but they that are sick.'

349 *fancy-monger*: One who deals in love (as a woodmonger deals in wood).

350 *quotidian*: Daily, recurrent fever.

356 *rushes*: Reeds. Rosalind is implying that it is easy to escape from the cage of love.

358 *blue eye*: Eye with dark rings around it.

359 *unquestionable*: Not to be spoken to.

361–2 *simply your having*: The little you have.

364 *unbanded*: Without a coloured hatband.

365–6 *careless desolation*: Despondency beyond caring.

367 *point-device*: Fastidiously precise (shortened from 'at point device', from French '*à point devis*').

374 *still*: Always.

376 *admired*: Marvelled at.

383 *merely*: Completely (similarly at 402, and cf. *mere oblivion* at II.7.166).

384 *dark house and a whip*: Rosalind is not inventing the punishment. This was a common Elizabethan treatment for the insane, as the trick played on Malvolio in *Twelfth Night* shows.

386 *ordinary*: Common, frequent.

392 *moonish*: Changeable (like the moon).

397 *entertain*: Receive kindly.

399 *that*: With the result that.

drave: Drove (a common form of the past tense).

400 *living*: Real, authentic, not put on for the occasion. (Othello asks for 'a living reason' of Desdemona's guilt, III.3.406.)

403 *liver*: This was thought to be the seat of the passions.

411–12 *by the way*: On the way.

III.3

3 *feature*: Form (or, judging by Touchstone's next lines, 'conduct'); but presumably Audrey suspects an innuendo.

4 *warrant*: Protect.

6–7 *capricious . . . Goths*: There is a series of learned puns here. *Capricious* is derived from the Latin word '*caper*' (goat) and originally meant 'goat-like' and 'lascivious'; *Goths* was pronounced like 'goats'; and Ovid, who was exiled from Rome and forced to live among the Goths, was renowned not for being *honest* (pure) but as the

author of some very licentious poems: indeed, his
banishment was possibly due either to his *Ars Amatoria*
or to his liaison with the Emperor's daughter Julia. All
this is wasted on Audrey, of course, but not on Jaques.

8 *ill-inhabited*: Badly housed.

8–9 *Jove in a thatched house*: Jaques also has his classical
learning. He refers to the time when Jove, in disguise,
visited the earth and was warmly entertained by the poor
old couple Baucis and Philemon, in their humble cottage.

11 *seconded with*: Supported by.

12–13 *it strikes . . . in a little room*: For the possible reference
to the death of Marlowe, see Introduction, p. xxxiii.
a little room may mean a private one in an inn, in which
the *reckoning* ('bill for a meal') would be more likely
to be unreasonable.

19 *may be said*: Mason's emendation 'it may be said'
perhaps makes the sense a little clearer, but Touchstone
is merely playing with words. There may be a pun on
feign meaning 'pretend' and 'fain' meaning 'desire'.

26 *hard-favoured*: Ugly.

29 *material*: Full of matter; or practical, unromantic.

35 *foul*: Perhaps to Audrey the word means only 'plain'
('homely' in the current American usage).

38–9 *Sir Oliver Martext*: *Martext* is a type-name, of the kind
frequently used in anti-Puritan pamphlets; and *Sir*
seems to have been the normal 'title' for an unlettered
country clergyman.

46 *horn-beasts*: There is the usual quibble on 'animals with
horns' and 'cuckolds'. F's *horne* may be a misreading
of 'hornd', but the sense is not affected.

46–7 *what though*: What of it?

51 *Poor men alone*: Whether one retains the F punctua-
tion (*euen so poore men alone:*) or interprets as in the
given text, the sense is clear: Touchstone himself raises,
and rejects, the supposition that only poor men's wives
are unfaithful.

52 *rascal*: Poorer deer of the herd.

58 *want*: Be without (but there is another learned quibble
because of the 'horn of plenty').

68 *'ild*: Reward (abbreviation of 'yield' in its original meaning). So too at V.4.53.

69 *your last company*: Your latest company ('your action in joining us now').

70 *toy*: Matter of no great importance.
be covered: Replace your hat. Here, and to William at V.1.16–17, Touchstone condescendingly speaks as the monarch or nobleman normally speaks to the inferior who has thus shown a mark of respect – but the respect was being paid by Jaques to the clergyman's office, not to Touchstone.

72 *bow*: Yoke (or part inserted in it).

79 *wainscot*: Wooden panelling.
panel: If, as has been suggested, *panel* could also mean 'prostitute', *warp* may also have the secondary meaning of 'go wrong'.

81 *not in the mind but*: This must be the double negative that does make an affirmative: 'inclined to think that'.

85 *me . . . thee*: Jaques's internal rhyme may be unintentional, but Touchstone caps it with a deliberate one *Audrey . . . bawdry*. F sets the lines out as verse.

89–95 *O sweet Oliver*: Touchstone sings part of, and parodies, a popular ballad, which is believed to have been sung to the tune of 'In peascod time'. See The Songs.

III.4

6 *dissembling colour*: Red; or, as 10 has it, *chestnut*: the traditional colour of Judas's hair and therefore the sign of hypocrisy.

10 *your chestnut*: Not Rosalind's but 'the chestnut we are talking about'.

13 *holy bread*: This was originally the bread that was blessed and distributed to those who had *not* taken Communion, but after the Reformation it came to mean sacramental bread. (Interestingly the phrase was expunged by a seventeenth-century Catholic priest censoring a copy of the second Folio to be used by English students at Valladolid in Spain.)

14 *cast lips of Diana*: Lips cast for a statue of Diana, the

goddess of chastity. (The alternative interpretation, 'cast off', seems almost ludicrous.)

15 *of winter's sisterhood*: That is to say, extremely 'cold' or chaste.

23 *concave*: Hollow.

28 *tapster*: Waiter, or drawer of ale, in an inn, who would also make up the *reckonings* ('bills').

32 *question*: Conversation.

34 *what*: Why.

36 *brave*: Fine.

36–40 *He … swears brave oaths … noble goose*: Orlando's oaths merely glance off the heart of his loved one, just as an insignificant (or, perhaps, 'unskilled') knight, who in tilting spurs his horse only on one side, breaks his lance like a coward, with a glancing blow (instead of hitting his target in the centre).

43 *complained of*: Uttered his lament about.

51 *remove*: Go, move off.

III.5

5 *Falls*: Drops.

6 *But first begs*: Without first begging.

11 *sure*: Surely.

13 *atomies*: Motes (as before at III.2.225).

23 *cicatrice and capable impressure*: Scar-like mark and perceptible imprint.

29 *fancy*: Love.

38–9 *no more in you … to bed*: Rosalind means that Phebe's beauty alone would not light up the room and make a candle unnecessary.

42 *ordinary*: Ordinary run.

43 *sale-work*: Ready-made goods (inferior to more careful work).

'Od's: An abbreviation of 'May God save'.

47 *bugle*: Bead-like. A bugle was a glass bead, usually black (and Phebe's eyes are black according to 130).

50 *south*: South wind.

51 *properer*: More handsome (as again at 55).

53 *ill-favoured*: Ugly.

61 *Cry the man mercy*: Beg the man's forgiveness.

62 *Foul is most foul ... a scoffer*: Ugliness is most ugly
when the ugliness is in being a scoffer (with 'wicked'
as a secondary meaning of *foul*).

66–7 *He's fallen ... my anger*: Some editors think these lines
are an aside, but Rosalind is not concerned to spare
Phebe's feelings.

69 *sauce*: Rebuke, sting.

78 *see*: See you.

79 *abused*: Deceived.

81 *saw*: Maxim. This is a quotation from Marlowe's *Hero
and Leander*. See Introduction, p. xxxiv.

89 *extermined*: Destroyed, ended.

90 *neighbourly*: In accordance with the injunction to love
one's neighbour as oneself.

93 *it is not that*: The time has not yet come.

95 *erst*: Not long ago.
   irksome: Hateful, offensive.

100 *in such a poverty of grace*: That is, because so little
grace has been shown, or given, to him.

104 *scattered*: Random.

107 *bounds*: Lands (on which he had the right of pasturage).

108 *carlot*: Peasant, churl. (The word is not recorded elsewhere, but 'carl' is, in the same sense.)

123 *damask*: The reference may be to the damask rose or
to the woven fabric.

125 *In parcels*: Feature by feature.

132 *answered not again*: Did not answer back.

133 *omittance is no quittance*: This is a proverb: 'Failure to
do something at the time is not a full discharge from
the responsibility of doing it in the long run.'

136 *straight*: Immediately.

138 *passing short*: Extremely curt.

IV.1

3 *melancholy fellow*: There is, no doubt, topical humour
here: a pose of melancholy seems to have been fashionable in the 1590s and early seventeenth century, and
many dramatists refer to it. The man who adopted the
pose could always claim that black bile predominated
in his make-up and made his 'humour' inevitable. (Cf.

humorous at 18.) Fashionable modern 'complexes' provide the perfect parallel.

6 *abominable*: The F spelling *abhominable* probably preserves the false etymology '*ab homine*' and so the second sense of 'not human'.

7 *modern*: Everyday (as at II.7.157).

8 *sad*: Solemn.

13 *politic*: Crafty, guided by considerations only of expediency.

14 *nice*: (Pretending to be) fastidious.

16 *simples*: Ingredients.

26 *travail*: (1) Work hard; (2) travel.

28 *Going*: F does not mark an 'exit' for Jaques, but obviously Rosalind should not deign to notice Orlando, who has come late for his appointment, until Jaques, who has begun to leave as he speaks his farewell, is offstage; she continues talking to Jaques as he goes.

30 *lisp*: Affect a foreign accent (Rosalind's list of complaints against returned travellers echoes many others in Elizabethan writing).
disable: Belittle.

33 *swam*: Floated (an alternative form of the past participle). The gibe has the further point that Venice was the goal of many Elizabethan travellers, partly because it was notorious for its prostitutes.

42–3 *clapped him o'th'shoulder*: Arrested him or claimed him as his own.

49 *jointure*: Marriage settlement.

55 *prevents*: Anticipates.
slander: Disgrace (rather than 'evil report' in the modern sense).

60 *leer*: Complexion (the restricted meaning 'sly look' seems to have developed later).

67 *gravelled*: Perplexed, at a loss (a similar modern image is 'stranded').

68 *out*: At a loss.

69 *warn*: Summon (although Onions and others believe it to be a variant of 'warrant').

77 *honesty*: Virtue, chastity.

ranker: More suspect (but some editors paraphrase as 'stronger').

78 *of*: Out of (and Rosalind proceeds to pun on *suit* in the senses of 'suit of clothes' and 'courting' and possibly even 'law suit').

85 *by attorney*: By proxy (as in 'power of attorney').

87 *videlicet*: Namely (Rosalind is continuing the legal language begun by *attorney* or *suit*).

89 *Grecian club*: There are various versions of how Troilus, the prototype of the true lover, met his death; this is Rosalind's own. (Shakespeare's *Troilus and Cressida* does not carry the story to the death of Troilus but has him fling himself recklessly into battle when he discovers Cressida to be false.)

90 *Leander*: According to the accepted version of the story, he swam the Hellespont every night to visit Hero in Sestos (and was drowned).

119 *Go to*: Not an abbreviation, but an exclamation of mild or simulated impatience.

127 *commission*: Authority. This exchange of vows may have had even greater significance for an Elizabethan audience, since such a declaration, before a third party, constituted one kind of legal marriage contract.

129 *goes before*: Anticipates (because, for one thing, she has not waited to be asked 'Will you . . .?').

139 *Barbary*: A breed introduced from Barbary, the 'Barb' (apparently its origin is enough to imply jealousy).

140 *against*: Anticipating, predicting.
new-fangled: Readily distracted by every novelty.

142 *Diana in the fountain*: A figure of Diana was the centre of more than one fountain. Shakespeare may or may not have been thinking of the one erected in London in 1596 (it does not seem to have had a *weeping* Diana).

150 *Make*: Close (a use still found in dialect).

155 *'Wit, whither wilt'*: For the same joke, see I.2.53–4 and note.

162 *her husband's occasion*: The opportunity of finding fault with her husband.

171 *but one cast away*: Only one woman cast off. (Editors

have suspected a proverb or quotation from a popular ballad.)

177 *pathetical*: Affecting; producing strong emotion (not only pity).

180 *gross*: Whole; or large.

185 *try*: Judge the case.

186 *simply misused*: Completely disgraced.

196 *bastard of Venus*: Cupid (son of Venus but by Mercury, not by her husband Vulcan).

197 *thought*: It is difficult to say which of many possible shades of meaning the word has here: probably 'fancy' rather than 'melancholy'.

spleen: Caprice, waywardness.

198 *abuses*: Deceives.

IV.2

This charming interlude, which contributes to the pastoral atmosphere (and mocks it), has the added function of marking the passing of the two hours specified in the previous scene.

0 *Lords dressed as foresters*: The F stage direction is *Enter Iaques and Lords, Forresters*. Lines 2 and 7 are given to *Lord* and the song is headed simply *Musicke, Song* with no singer named. Perhaps this time foresters were intended to appear and even to sing, but there would seem to be no need for variation from II.1 and II.7: the Lords would have done the hunting and Jaques could address one of them as *forester* because of the costume. It is not necessary to give Amiens either line 7 or the song, for Jaques's lines 8–9 may envisage singing by the whole group.

12–13 *the rest shall bear ... This burden*: *burden* does also mean 'chorus' (cf. III.2.240 and note) and some editors take these words to be a direction to *the rest* to sing the refrain. But F prints the words in italic, as part of the song; *bear* rhymes with *wear* although F prints *Then sing ... burthen* as one line; and the point of the song is that *all* must run the risk of cuckoldry.

18 *lusty*: This time there is reference to 'lust' in the modern

sense: the horn is *lusty* because it is the symbol of the wife's lust as well as the husband's shame.

IV.3

2 *much*: Used ironically: cf. the modern colloquialism 'a fat lot of . . .'

18 *phoenix*: The point is that only one phoenix, according to the myth, could be alive at any one time; the new bird rose from the ashes of its predecessor.

'Od's my will: As God's is my will (or 'God save my will').

24 *turned*: Brought.

26 *freestone*: A fine-grained limestone or sandstone, between brown and yellow in colour.

35 *giant rude*: This is probably a compound adjective: 'incredibly barbarous, on the scale of a giant'.

40 *Phebes me*: Addresses me in her own style.

45 *laid apart*: Doffed for the time being.

49 *vengeance*: Damage.

50 *Meaning me a beast*: Thereby making me into a beast (since my eye has a different effect from a man's).

51 *eyne*: Eyes (an old form, used by Shakespeare here as a 'poeticism').

54 *aspect*: Possibly 'look' but more probably this is the astrological term, meaning, roughly, 'phase'.

59 *by him seal up thy mind*: Use him as messenger to carry a sealed letter in which you state your decision. The alternative explanation, 'make your final decision', hardly explains *by him*.

60 *kind*: Disposition.

62 *make*: Bring with me; or do.

79 *bottom*: Valley.

80 *rank of osiers*: Row of willows.

81 *Left*: Passed. But see Introduction, p. xlvi.

87 *favour*: Complexion; or countenance.

bestows himself: Carries himself, has the manner.

88 *ripe sister*: Mature older sister (of the girl Celia). Some editors emend *sister* to 'forester', not very plausibly.

low: Short (or 'shorter' if *low and browner* is to be construed, in a normal Elizabethan way, as 'lower and browner').

94 *napkin*: Handkerchief.

102 *fancy*: Love.

113 *indented*: Zigzagging, undulating.

117 *When that*: For the time when.

123 *render*: Declare, describe (as).

129 *kindness*: Probably in both senses: (1) kinship; (2) generosity.

130 *just occasion*: Legitimate excuse, or perfect opportunity.

132 *hurtling*: Tumult, violent conflict.

135 *contrive*: Scheme.

139 *By and by*: Immediately (the sense is much weaker now).

141 *recountments*: Narratives of our adventures (the word is the grammatical object of *bathed*).

144 *entertainment*: Hospitality.

151 *Brief*: In brief (as at 143).
    recovered: Revived.

166 *a body*: Anybody, one.

170 *passion of earnest*: Genuine emotion or suffering.

V.I

10 *clown*: Yokel, country bumpkin.

12 *shall be flouting*: Must jeer.
    hold: Refrain.

13 *even*: F's spelling *eu'n* may represent a rustic speech, which Touchstone imitates.

14 *God ye*: God give you.

34 *lips to open*: Perhaps William's mouth is similarly wide open, but with astonishment.

40 *figure*: Accepted device (such as hyperbole). Touchstone's illustration, of course, is deliberate nonsense.

42 *consent*: Agree.
    ipse: Latin for 'he himself'.

51 *to wit*: That is to say (a legal phrase).

53 *bastinado*: Beating with a cudgel (as against fencing with *steel*).

54 *bandy with thee in faction*: Compete against you in insults and other forms of dissension.

55 *policy*: 'Machiavellian' policy (using any means to achieve the desired end).

V.2

4 *persever*: An obsolete form of 'persevere', stressed on the second syllable.

5 *giddiness*: Rashness.

11 *estate*: Settle.

14 *all's*: All his.

26 *sound*: Swoon.

28 *where you are*: What you are referring to.

30 *thrasonical*: In the bragging style of the soldier Thraso, in Terence's *Eunuch* (Shakespeare was certainly not the first to use the word).

36 *degrees*: There is a quibble on *degrees* meaning also flight (*pair*) of stairs, and another on *incontinent*: (1) in haste; (2) unchaste.

39 *clubs*: Some editors see a reference to the Elizabethan custom of calling 'clubs' when summoning help to break up a street brawl.

50 *Know of me then . . .*: Although some wrong conclusions have been drawn, it has rightly been noted that Rosalind's style changes here to a manner much more formal – some would no doubt say 'ritualistic' – as she begins to adopt the role of manipulator of events. The syntax becomes more involved, the sentences longer – and the audience knows that the time for joking is now over.

51–2 *conceit*: Understanding.

53 *insomuch*: In as much as.

56 *grace me*: Add to my own merits or reputation.

58 *conversed*: Associated (or even 'studied').

59 *not damnable*: Not eligible for damnation (his is not 'black' magic, involving the devil). A magician of the wrong kind might be condemned to death too (hence 67–8).

60 *gesture*: Demeanour.

63 *inconvenient*: Inappropriate, out of place.

64–5 *human as she is*: In the flesh ('the real Rosalind, not the mere phantom or spirit that you might expect a magician to conjure up').

67 *tender*: Value.

69 *bid*: Invite.

74 *study*: Aim.

75 *despiteful*: Contemptuous.

89 *fantasy*: Imagination not controlled by reason.

91 *observance*: Humble attention. The repetition of the word at 93 may be an error – compositor's or author's (in which case one has the hopeless task of guessing what Shakespeare may have written or intended to write) – but it is just possible that *all observance* is the best Silvius can do to sum up what he has been saying.

104–5 *howling of Irish wolves*: The phrase is perhaps an adaptation of one in Lodge, where Rosalynde tells Montanus that in courting Phoebe he barks 'with the wolves of Syria against the moon' (that is, in vain). Perhaps Shakespeare's wolves are Irish because of the tradition that once a year the Irish were turned into wolves.

V.3

4 *dishonest*: Unchaste – with a pun, not intended by Audrey – on *woman of the world*, which she uses in its other meaning of 'married woman'. Perhaps there are subtle allusions to Genesis 19:31 and Luke 20:34. *dishonest* is the opposite of *honest* as used two lines later to mean 'honourable'.

10 *clap into't roundly*: Strike into it without unnecessary preliminaries.

10–11 *hawking*: Making the customary noises to clear the throat.

11–12 *the only prologues*: Merely the prologues.

13 *in a tune*: This may mean either 'keeping time with one another' or 'in unison'.

15–38 *It was a lover* . . . : The best-known setting for this song is that by Shakespeare's famous contemporary Thomas Morley (published in his *First Book of Airs*, 1600, of which there is a unique copy in the Folger Shakespeare Library; see The Songs). If Morley wrote the music especially for Shakespeare's words (as seems likely from his statement in the Dedication that the airs 'were made this vacation time'), this would be the only known occasion when a Shakespeare song was so set by one of the great school of Elizabethan lutenists;

but it is possible that Morley's music (and even the words) preceded the play. The Morley version justifies the reordering of the stanzas as in the text (F prints the present last stanza as the second) and the emending of F's *rang time* to *ring time*: perhaps it would also justify the omitting of *the* at 18 (*In the spring time*) to make that part of the first stanza identical with the others (Morley has notes of music only for *In* and *spring*). At 23 it reads not *country folks* but *Countrie fooles* and at 17 has the tempting reading *corne fields*; on the other hand, it confirms *a life* (as against the emendation 'life') at 29.

18 *ring time*: Time for giving or exchanging rings.

21 *Between the acres of the rye*: (Presumably) on the unploughed strips dividing the fields of rye.

35 *the prime*: Perfection (but 'the prime' also meant 'the spring').

40 *the ditty*: The words (as opposed to the *note* or music).

41 *untuneable*: Touchstone probably means 'unmusical, even though the words weren't hard to set' or 'ill fitted to the words, insignificant as they were'; but the Pages reply as if he meant either that they both failed to keep proper time or that they did not sing in tune with each other.

V.4

1 *fear they hope, and know they fear*: Fear that they are only hoping against hope, and know in their hearts that they are afraid.

5 *urged*: Stated formally, and clarified.

18 *make all this matter even*: Smooth everything out (perhaps with an implied contrast between even and odd). The phrase is curiously echoed at 25 and again by Hymen at 106.

21 *Keep you ... marry me*: It is not true that one has to pronounce *Phebe* as one syllable in order to scan this line, which may be basically trochaic, with a stress on *your*.

27 *lively*: Lifelike; or vivid.

touches: Traits; or strokes (a metaphor from painting).

favour: Appearance, features, look.

32 *desperate*: Dangerous.

34 *Obscurèd*: Concealed, and protected (as the magician is protected from interference by devils while he is within his magic circle).

35 *toward*: On the way.

36 *a pair*: The reference is to Genesis 7:2: the Lord told Noah to take with him into the ark seven of each species of 'clean' beast – but 'of unclean cattle two, the male and his female'.

40 *motley-minded*: With mind as mixed as the thread of his coat.

42–3 *put me to my purgation*: Give me the chance of clearing myself (cf. I.3.51 and note).

43 *measure*: A formal aristocratic dance.

44 *politic*: Machiavellian (cf. *policy* at V.1.55).

45 *undone*: By not paying them.

46 *like to have fought*: Almost fought (the joke being, of course, that courtiers seldom stand to their words when a quarrel becomes serious).

47 *ta'en up*: Made up (with the consequent avoiding of the duel). The phrase is used again at 95–6.

53 *'ild*: Reward (as at III.3.68).
   desire you of the like: This has been variously interpreted: 'I ask permission to return the compliment' or 'I sincerely hope you do think so (and will continue to think so)'.

54–5 *copulatives*: Those about to be joined, in marriage and carnally.

56 *blood breaks*: Passion wanes.

58 *honesty*: Chastity.

61 *swift and sententious*: Quick-witted and full of wisdom.

62 *fool's bolt*: There is a proverb 'a fool's bolt is soon shot'; and perhaps Touchstone is even alluding to the form of bolt or short arrow that was known as a 'quarrel'.

63 *dulcet diseases*: Commentators have tripped over the phrase, but it probably means 'mild or pleasant weaknesses' and refers to the fool's inability to forbear from gibes.

67 *seeming*: Becomingly.
68 *dislike*: Express disapproval of.
69–70 *in the mind*: Of the opinion that.
73 *disabled*: Belittled (as at IV.1.30).
78–9 *Circumstantial*: Indirect, the product of circumstance only.
84 *measured*: That is, to see that one was not longer than the other (a necessary precaution before the duel).
87 *in print*: There is a quibble here. The phrase also meant 'in a precise way', as did 'by the book': according to the textbook, 'according to Hoyle'. There were textbooks setting out the justifications for duelling, and Shakespeare possibly has a particular one in mind.
95–6 *take up*: Settle.
98–9 *swore brothers*: Pledged themselves to act like brothers, ever after.
103 *stalking-horse*: The horse or, more frequently, imitation horse behind which the hunter sheltered without disturbing the quarry.
104 *presentation*: The *Oxford English Dictionary* takes this as an example of *presentation* meaning a theatrical or symbolic representation or show. It could also mean 'inferior representation', 'mere shadow of the real thing' – and the Duke is saying that Touchstone's folly is only pretended.
     Hymen: The god of marriage, who was frequently represented in masques. F has simply *Enter Hymen* ... and the director must make up his mind who plays the part. Some editors think it should be given to the singer who earlier plays Amiens (F does not specify that Hymen's first words are to be sung but does print them in italic). If, as others have maintained, although unnecessarily, the masque was written into the play for a special performance at a wedding, one of the distinguished guests may have been brought in as Hymen. But too much fuss altogether has been made over the masque: it is an appropriate way of arranging weddings, and the stilted verse is not un-Shakespearian but is in the manner of his other masques and interludes, in,

for example, *Cymbeline* and *Timon of Athens*.

104 *Still music*: Quiet, peaceful music (such as that of recorders and flutes, not drums and trumpets).

106 *made even*: See 18 and note.

107 *Atone together*: Are joined as one, come into accord.

111–12 *her hand . . . her bosom*: The F reading, *his* in both places, can be justified, if at all, on the ground that Rosalind is still being referred to as a boy. F does not *say* that Rosalind appears in female dress here but the Duke and Orlando – and Phebe – obviously now first see her as a woman.

122 *bar*: Stop.

127 *holds true contents*: Commentators find the phrase feeble, or incomprehensible, but presumably it means 'if the couples are to remain true to their vows, to what they have alleged to be true'.

128 *cross*: Trial or affliction.

130 *accord*: Consent.

132 *sure together*: Bound fast.

141 *High*: Line 142 suggests that this may mean 'highly' rather than 'true'.

145 *Even daughter*: The phrase is unusual, whether addressed to Celia ('even as a daughter', 'no less than a daughter') or to Rosalind ('and you, my true daughter').

153 *Addressed*: Gathered, prepared.
power: Armed force.

154 *In his own conduct*: Under his own leadership.

157 *religious man*: Man of some religious function or intent (probably a hermit).

158 *question*: Discussion.

161 *them*: The F reading is *him*, which has been defended on the ground that it was for Duke Senior to restore the lands to the owners if he wished.

163 *engage*: Pledge.

164 *offerest fairly*: Bringest splendid gifts and offerings.

166 *potent*: Perhaps not 'powerful' but 'potential': Orlando will inherit it.

167 *do those ends*: Achieve the aims.

170 *shrewd*: Sharp (a possible reference back to the winter wind and its *icy fang*).

172 *states*: Status, rank.

176 *measures*: Stately dances (as at 43 and again at 190),
but with a quibble on *With measure* earlier in the line,
where it means 'in good measure', 'liberally'. (At 172
measure has one of its normal modern meanings.)

177 *Sir*: Jaques addresses the Duke, asking his pardon for
interrupting and for addressing another directly.

179 *thrown into neglect*: Rejected as worthless.
pompous: Full of pomp.

198 *good wine needs no bush*: This is a proverb ('what is
good needs no advertisement'), alluding to the
vintner's practice of hanging a 'bush' (generally, some
ivy) outside his shop.

203 *insinuate with you*: Subtly work on you and win you
over.

204 *furnished*: Dressed (as also at III.2.238).

205 *conjure you*: Work on you by charms or spells, like a
magician.

211 *If I were a woman*: The part of Rosalind was, of course,
played by a boy – and, characteristically, Shakespeare
takes advantage of the fact.

213 *liked*: Appealed to, pleased.
defied: Disdained.

216 *bid me farewell*: Grant the applause that will allow me
to leave the stage in good spirits.

Read more in Penguin

PENGUIN SHAKESPEARE